BEAD & WIRE
FASHION
JEWELRY

JESSICA ROSE

BEAD & WIRE
FASHION
JEWELRY

A collection of stunning statement pieces to make

THE GUILD OF MASTER CRAFTSMAN
PUBLICATIONS

First published 2014 by
Guild of Master Craftsman Publications Ltd
Castle Place, 166 High Street, Lewes,
East Sussex BN7 1XU

Text © Jessica Rose, 2014
Copyright in the Work © GMC Publications Ltd, 2014

All photographs by Jessica Rose except for those credited on page 174.

ISBN 978 1 86108 967 0

Publisher Jonathan Bailey
Production Manager Jim Bulley
Managing Editor Gerrie Purcell
Senior Project Editor Dominique Page
Editor Nicky Gyopari
Managing Art Editor Gilda Pacitti
Designer Chloë Alexander

Set in Roboto and Didot
Colour origination by GMC Reprographics
Printed and bound in China

CONTENTS

Introduction   8

Tools & Materials

Tools   14
Materials   17

Techniques

Making a loop   26
Threading beads with wire   29
Making earwires   30
Making clasps   33
Making a coil   34
Jumprings   37
Using headpins   38
Wrapping a briolette   41
Making swirls   42
Making wire charms   45
Crimping   49

Statement Necklaces

Coral glow	53
Sea breeze	59
Paradise	65
Chain attraction	71
Forbidden glamour	79

Designer Earrings

Fiesta	89
Pearl luster	95
Spring burst	99
Purple haze	105

Couture Bracelets

Love hurts	115
Beach babe	119
Luxury lace	125
Aladdin's treasure	131
Friends forever	141

Blinging Rings

Destiny	151
Candy	157
Glamour	161
Entwined	167

Suppliers and resources	172
About the author	173
Picture acknowledgments	174
Index	175

INTRODUCTION

Making beautiful jewelry doesn't have to involve lots of expensive tools and machinery anymore. Almost anyone can design and make their own stunning collections of necklaces, bracelets, earrings, and rings from home with a few basic tools, techniques, and a splash of inspiration. This book shows you how to do just that. After covering the fundamentals you will be guided through 18 fashion-focused projects that are designed to stand out—projects that even a complete beginner can master. They all incorporate beads and wire, which are some of the best materials to use to make professional jewelry from home. They are easy to get hold of and once you know a few little tricks, you can make virtually anything with them!

Making it your own

One of the best things about making your own jewelry is that it can match your unique style. All the techniques and projects in this book are designed with that in mind—as your confidence increases you will be encouraged to experiment and design collections that say something distinctive about you.

> *" Fashion is not something that exists in dresses only, fashion is in the sky, in the street. Fashion has to do with ideas, the way we live, what is happening. "*
>
> COCO CHANEL

Trend spotting

Making jewelry inspired by fashion isn't all about the latest look. Yes there are seasons, colors, and innovations in the fast-paced world of fashion that inspire us, but you can also look at fashion through the ages, items of jewelry that have withstood the test of time, even inside your own wardrobe, to figure out what your style is and how the jewelry you make and design can reflect that.

When looking at current trends there are a few tips to get you started:

- Browse magazines. Fashion magazines, women's magazines, and lifestyle magazines will all give you ideas for what is current.
- Watch the latest movies. What are they about? What jewelry can you see being worn?
- What are celebrities wearing at the moment? Has any of their jewelry been in the news?
- Go to art galleries and museums for inspiration. Mixing old and new styles can be a great look.
- Visit clothes shops. Notice color trends, patterns, and designs for that season and use them to generate ideas in your making.

- Look for inspiration online. There are tons of fashion and style blogs with beautiful images and ideas you can work from. Pinterest is a designer's dream tool, as it is somewhere you can collate all your images and make a collection of mood boards. Be warned—Pinterest is addictive, but it's so worth it!

Once you start trend spotting, there will be no stopping you.

Creating a mood board

A mood board is a great tool to help you formulate your ideas, and you will see how I've used them throughout this book. Essentially, it is a collage of all the things that have provided inspiration. It might include colors, a picture of a particular outfit, bag, or shoes, a texture, fabric, or beads. It could also include sketches, photographs, or anything else you might associate with the piece or collection you are designing. Once the ideas are collated you can start to build up a concept of the piece of jewelry you would like to make.

The advantage of creating a mood board is that you can get an idea of what the jewelry might look like and who it would suit. It is especially useful if you are making a collection, as it can highlight elements that all the pieces in the collection have in common. So, when making a set of necklaces, earrings, bracelets, and rings you can keep them grounded in the mood board but each piece will still have its own unique design.

Making jewelry to sell

If you are planning to sell your jewelry, either to a shop or the general public, you need to have your intended audience in mind from the start. Consider the cost of the materials you are using, as this will affect the price of the finished piece. Think also about what type of jewelry your ideal customer would want to wear.

For most jewelers, the best way to start selling is to make pieces for friends and family. Then you can receive referrals from them and gradually figure out what sells well and what is unique about the pieces you design that makes people want to buy them.

Whatever your reason for making jewelry, the first stage is to learn the basics and get to grips with the tools and materials. So, without further ado, let's get started.

TOOLS & MATERIALS

TOOLS

You will need a basic tool kit to make the projects in this book; the tools don't need to be specialist or expensive and are sold by most jewelry-making stores.

Pliers

Pliers are essential in jewelry making. Once you have mastered the basics with them, you will become firm friends. You will need the following types:

Round-nose

At the end of these pliers are two tapered cone shapes. They are used for making wire loops and circles. **(1)**

Chain-nose

Also known as snipe-nose, these pliers are flat on the inside and pointed on the outside. They are perfect for squashing things and getting into those tight, hard-to-reach places. **(2)**

Flat-nose

These are flat on the inside and outside and have a rectangular edge. They are often used for bending or straightening wire and opening and closing jumprings. **(3)**

Side cutters

Also known simply as cutters, these act like scissors. Having a flat edge on one side and a beveled edge on the other, they are used to cut wires—providing a nice flush cut when needed. **(4)**

Needle file

A mini metal file, perfect for curving sharp wire ends. **(5)**

Wooden mandrel

This tapered stick is used to shape ring bases. **(6)**

General and fabric-cutting scissors

A really sharp pair of fabric-cutting **(7)** scissors is required for working with leather, suede, and lace. Keep them separate from your general scissors **(8)** so they don't become blunted.

Paintbrushes

You will need a couple of fine paintbrushes for applying glue and paint to your jewelry. **(9)**

Bead mat

This is a fabric sheet with tiny fibers that stick upward, holding your beads still while you work with them. **(10)**

A mug

A cup or mug, or other cylindrical objects, in different sizes are ideal for shaping wires around. **(11)**

Steel block and hammer

These are used to harden wire and add texture to it; however, they are not essential for this book. **(12 & 13)**

MATERIALS

All the materials you need to make the pieces in this book can be easily sourced from craft, bead, or jewelry-making shops, as well as from a multitude of online stores.

Beads

Beads can add color and shape to all types of jewelry and form the main feature of many of the projects in this book. They come in many shapes, sizes, types, and weights. One thing to look out for is the size of the hole in the middle of the bead, as you'll need to make sure the bead will fit onto your chosen stringing material before designing the piece. This is particularly important when you are using a thick stringing material such as elastic. Here are some of the most common bead types you will be using:

Shapes

- Round
- Oval
- Faceted
- Rondelle beads, which are slightly flattened, round beads and often faceted
- Nuggets
- Briolettes, which are pear-shaped, top-drilled beads and usually faceted
- Seed beads, which are tiny round beads
- Teardrop
- Bicones, which are a diamond-like shape. Swarovski are known for their trademark bicone glass beads

Types

- Acrylic
- Glass
- Semi-precious
- Swarovski
- Pearl
- Metal

Sizes

- Large focal beads
- Range of mid-sized beads
- Small spacer beads
- Seed beads

TIPS FOR BUYING BEADS

1 If buying online, always check the sizes. Keep a ruler to hand and draw them out if needed. They can look very big in pictures!

2 Check out your local bead shops or craft stores. I love buying beads in person; it is like going into a sweet shop. So pay them a visit before you start making.

3 Make a shopping list. Once you know what you need for your designs, write it down; it helps you to keep focus when you are buying your beads, as it is easy to get distracted in a bead shop!

Findings

"Findings" is the umbrella term given to a range of small metal components that hold your jewelry together. There are various types of finding that you will need to use in your jewelry making.

Headpins

These are short pieces of wire with stoppers on the end to prevent beads falling off. They can be flat-ended, ball-ended, or swirls. **(1)**

Earwire

This is the part of the earring that is inserted in your ear. It's also referred to as an earhook or earring finding. There are various types of earwire available to purchase. Alternatively you can make your own (see page 30). **(2)**

Clasps

These findings secure sections of a necklace or bracelet together. There are many types of clasp, including lobster clasps and bolt ring clasps, and you can also create your own (see page 32). **(3)**

Crimps and cord ends

A crimp is a tiny metal bead that is used for joining elements together. It comes in a range of sizes. Cord ends are useful for attaching ribbon and feathers to jewelry. **(4)**

Jumprings

These circles of metal, which usually have a split in the middle, are used to connect the different elements of an item of jewelry together. They are available in a range of sizes, or you can easily make your own (see page 36). **(5)**

Charms and elements

Cast elements and charms can be bought to attach to your pieces. They come in different designs, shapes, metals, and sizes. You can also make your own (see pages 44–47). **(6)**

Wire

Wire is used in jewelry making for all types of projects and can even be used to make your own findings. It comes in various shapes, including round, square, and half-round. **(7)**

The thickness of wire is measured in millimeters in the UK and Europe and in gauge in the USA. A common measurement used in the US is AWG, which stands for American Wire Gauge, which in this book is simply stated as US gauge. SWG stands for Standard Wire Gauge, which is sometimes used too and is therefore included throughout. The chart below shows some of the more common thicknesses of wire. For most of the projects in this book you will need to use US 20 gauge (SWG 21, 0.8mm) gold-plated or silver-plated wire.

AWG	MM	SWG
10	2.5mm	12
12	2mm	14
14	1.5mm	16
16	1.25mm	18
18	1mm	19
20	0.8mm	21
22	0.6mm	23
24	0.5mm	25
26	0.4mm	27
28	0.3mm	30

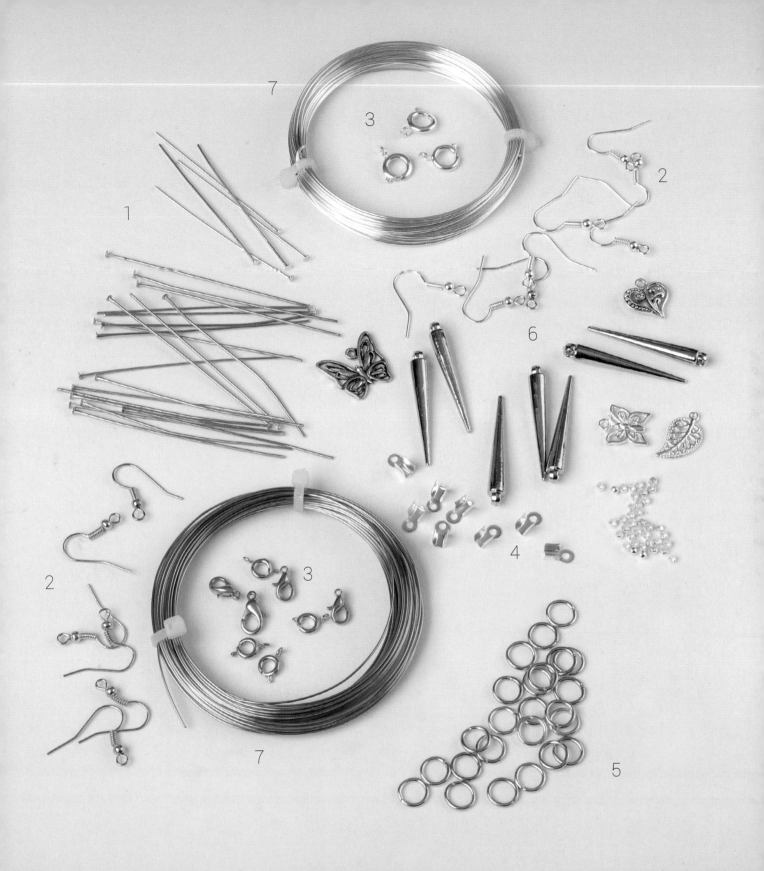

Metal types for findings and wire

There are many types of wire available. The wires used for the projects in this book are stated at the beginning of each project. However, when you are first learning how to make jewelry it is best to use copper or plated wires, because they are the least expensive.

Copper

This is inexpensive, yet very attractive. But be warned: water and copper do not mix—it leaves a green mark on the skin.

Silver-plated

This wire usually has copper or brass underneath and is coated in a layer of silver. It's great for fashion pieces but over time the plating can wear off.

Gold-plated

As above but coated in a layer of gold.

Sterling silver

This is solid silver, so it is more expensive, but it has a longer life span than plated.

Vermeil

Sterling silver that is plated in gold.

Gold

Solid gold wire or findings can be bought in 9ct or 18ct (sometimes also 14ct or 22ct) but it is expensive. Note the lower the carat number, the tougher the wire.

Gold-filled

A good alternative to solid gold findings. Gold-filled pieces have a thick layer of plating that won't wear off in the same way as gold-plated.

Colored wire

Also know as craft wire, it comes in lots of different colors, which can be fun to experiment with.

Other metals

Wire and findings are also available in brass and other base metals.

Stringing materials

You can use a range of materials to string beads and other elements. The following are some of the most popular:

Nylon

Thick nylon cord is hugely versatile and commonly used for threading beads.

Elastic/stretchy nylon

Great for stretchy bracelets or rings.

Colored waxed cord

Used a lot in friendship-style bracelets and adds color to your pieces.

Needle and thread

Self-explanatory, but yes, on occasion, a needle and thread is used in jewelry making.

Chain

Chain looks lovely incorporated in all types of fashion jewelry and there are lots of different types available to buy. Some of the most popular ones include curb chain, which tends to be a fairly thick, slightly edgy chain with curved links, and trace chain, which is a very fine chain for a delicate piece. Other chains include oval-linked, round-linked, and even square-linked.

Fabric

In this book fabrics, including leather, suede, and lace, are incorporated in some of the projects. Fabric can be glued or attached to jewelry with wire or sewn with thread. Keep in mind that fabric is not waterproof and can get dirty so materials that shrink, like leather, should not get wet.

Feathers

Feathers look striking in jewelry and are fairly simple to use. They come in all shapes and sizes, so feel free to experiment. You will mainly be using medium-sized dyed spotted feathers and stripped coque feathers for the projects in this book.

Bits and buttons

In between beads, chain, wire, and feathers you can add some other bits and pieces to great effect, including the following:

Buttons

Everyone has a spare tub of buttons somewhere and there is no better way to put it to good use than by using them to embellish your jewelry pieces.

Cabochons

These are flat-backed stones with a curved front that sit in settings that are made for them or in some cases are glued onto your pieces.

Flat-backed mounted crystals

You can buy all sorts of flat-backed crystals or stones to adorn your pieces, such as the flat-backed mounded gems used to make the statement ring on page 161.

Paints

In some of the projects in this book acrylic paints are used to add color and style to your piece.

Glues and adhesives

I'll let you into a little secret. Lots of jewelry is made using glue. For jewelers, it often feels like you are cheating, but in some cases it is the best thing for the job.

White (PVA) glue

This glue is easy to source and use, and it dries clear so it's perfect for if you put a little too much on.

UHU

This is an all-purpose adhesive that is stronger than white (PVA) glue and works well with fabrics.

Superglue

For when you need a really strong join and precise application, you can't go wrong with superglue.

Masking tape

Masking tape is great for temporarily holding cord or wire in place before gluing permanently.

TECHNIQUES

MAKING A LOOP

Creating loops in wire is a fundamental technique in jewelry making that allows you to connect pieces together and create part of larger wire findings and structures. Follow the steps below to make a perfect wire loop; and remember, if you don't get it right first time keep going—the more you do, the easier they become.

Step 1 Take a length of wire. I have used US 18 gauge (SWG 19, 1mm) gold plated.

Step 2 Place the end of the wire into your round-nose pliers so there is as little wire as possible sticking out the other side.

Step 3 Grip the pliers to hold the wire firmly with one hand while using a finger from the other hand to gently guide the wire around one side of the pliers.

Step 4 Keep pushing with your finger all the way up and over to make a single loop, then stop.

Step 5 Take the wire out of your pliers and you will probably notice that you have made a loop but that it is not completely closed. Instead, there is a small gap.

Step 6 To close the gap, place your wire back over one of the sides of the pliers and apply a little pressure from your finger to draw the gap closed.

Step 7 Now take the loop off the pliers and you will have a complete loop. You will notice that the loop is facing one side like a number 9.

Step 8 In order to centralize the loop (should you need to) put the end of your round-nose pliers through the loop so that one side is in the middle of the loop and the other side is on the outside, opposite to where the end of your wire meets the start of the circle.

Step 9 While gripping that in place, gently push the long length of wire with your finger down toward the jaw of your pliers that is on the outside of the main loop. Sometimes this step will open up the initial loop a bit. If so, just go back in with the pliers and close it.

Step 10 Remove the loop from the pliers and you should have a centralized wire loop.

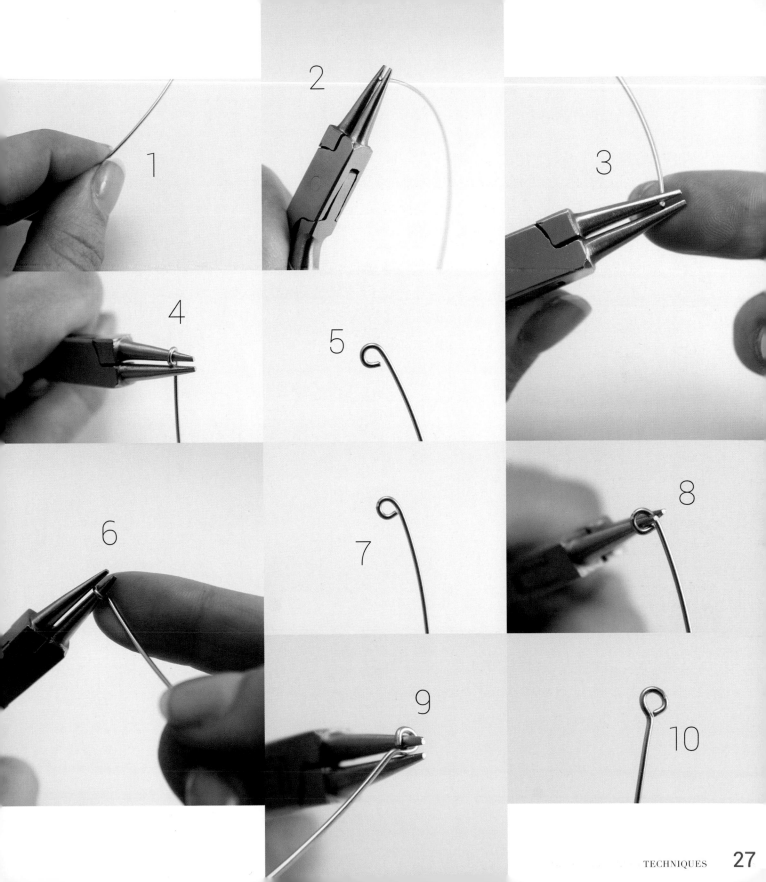

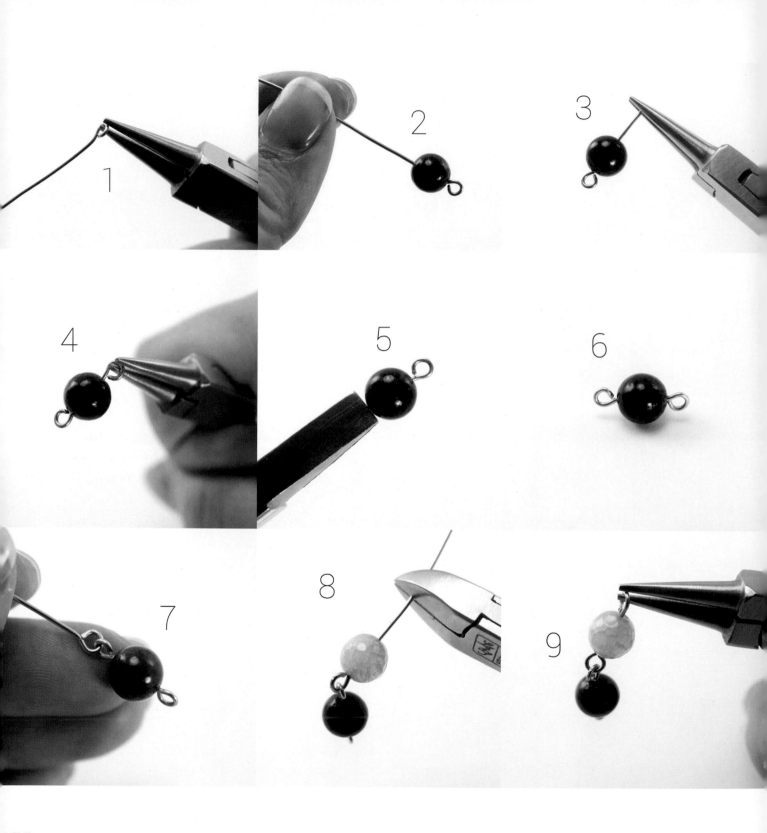

THREADING BEADS WITH WIRE

You don't need fancy findings to incorporate beads in your jewelry; instead you can use wire to make lots of fun and creative projects. The first thing you need to master is how to thread beads on to wire. This foundation technique is perfect for making simple necklaces, bracelets, and earrings and will lead you on to making many other types of jewelry.

Step 1 Take a length of US 20 gauge (SWG 21, 0.8mm) wire. Use your round-nose pliers to make a small loop at the end of the wire and centralize the loop with your pliers. (See page 26 for how to make a loop.)

Step 2 Thread a bead onto the end of the wire. The loop should act as a stopper to hold it in place.

Step 3 Cut the end of the wire approximately ³/₈in (10mm) above the bead then place the end of the wire in your round-nose pliers.

Step 4 Make a loop in the wire that goes down to meet the top of the bead. Centralize the loop by holding the bead and using the pliers to gently reposition it if needed.

Step 5 If you find the two loops at either end of your piece are facing different directions, hold one loop in your flat-nose pliers and the other in your chain-nose pliers, and twist them together until they are facing the right direction.

Step 6 You should now have a bead with a loop at either end that can be attached to an earring, necklace, or bracelet. If you want to add more beads, follow the next three steps.

Step 7 Take a new piece of wire and make a loop in the end. Open the loop slightly using your round-nose pliers and thread a loop from one end of your bead onto the new wire loop. Close the loop using your round-nose pliers.

Step 8 Thread a second bead onto the new piece of wire. Cut the wire off ³/₈in (10mm) above the bead.

Step 9 Make a loop as before to finish. You can continue in this way, adding as many beads as you like, looping them at each end.

MAKING EARWIRES

Earwires, also know as earhooks or sometimes "earring findings," are very useful to be able to make and are surprisingly simple to do with wire. Although you can buy earwires, making your own gives your pieces a more bespoke, handmade appearance. Once you have mastered the technique, you can experiment with different shapes and sizes. Using a thinner pen to shape the wire will give a smaller hoop while a thick marker pen can give a nice, big-looped wire.

Step 1 Take a piece of US 20 gauge (SWG 21, 0.8mm) gold- or silver-plated wire. Place the end of the wire into a pair of round-nose pliers around ¼in (5mm) from the end of the plier jaws. Make sure there is little or no wire sticking out the other side.

Step 2 Guide the wire around the pliers to make a loop.

Step 3 Place the looped wire onto a thick pen with the loop facing upward.

Step 4 While holding it in place with one hand, use the other hand to guide the wire around the pen to make a giant loop in the opposite direction. Take the wire round until it nearly touches the original loop at the back.

Step 5 Remove the wire from the pen and you should have a wire shape that consists of a small loop facing one direction followed by a large loop in the other direction.

Step 6 Using side cutters, cut the straight end of the wire to just below the small loop and use a needle file or small file to gently curve the sharp end of the wire, as this is the section that will be going through your ear.

Step 7 Once filed, slightly flick the end of the wire away from the rest of the piece using the end of your round-nose pliers. Then repeat all the steps to make a second earwire. You can leave the earwire making there or carry on to step 8 for a variation.

Step 8 If you wish to stylize your earwires and make them stronger, take a steel block and gently hammer the large curve on the wires. You only need to do a few strokes with the hammer to achieve this. It will give a nice hammered effect to the piece and work-harden the wire, making it stronger.

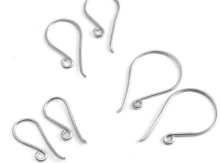

MAKING CLASPS

Clasps join the two ends of a necklace or bracelet securely together, usually at the back or side. You can buy them in all shapes and sizes, but it is handy to be able to make your own. With a bit of practice you'll be able to make them in just a few simple steps.

Hook-shaped clasp (top)

Step 1 Create a small loop at the end of a length of US 20 gauge (SWG 21, 0.8mm) or US 18 gauge (SWG 19, 1mm) wire. There's no need to centralize the loop; leave it facing to one side. Place the wire into a pair of round-nose pliers with the loop sitting just above the pliers and the wire tail protruding below.

Step 2 Gripping the pliers with one hand, use your other hand to guide the wire tail up and round the circular pliers in the opposite direction to the way the original loop is facing.

Step 3 Once the wires are touching at the back, take the wire off the pliers and cut it down before gently flicking the end of the wire with your chain-nose pliers.

Step 4 File the end gently using a needle file. The "hook clasp" is then complete. Team it with a jumpring on the other side to make a full, useable clasp for necklaces or bracelets.

Step 5 To connect the clasp to your jewelry, simply open the small original loop slightly using your round-nose pliers, thread on the end of the piece you are making, then close it tightly again using the pliers. Add a jumpring (see page 37) to the other end of your piece for the clasp to hook into.

S-shaped clasp (bottom)

Step 1 To create a fancier, s-shaped clasp, you begin in the same way: make a small loop, followed by an opposite-facing larger loop, as for a hook-shaped clasp.

Step 2 Place the whole piece back into your round-nose pliers at the bottom of the plier jaws and hold it firmly closed. Make sure the original loop is right up against the pliers.

Step 3 Using your fingers, pull the wire up and over the pliers in the opposite direction to the way the last large loop you created is facing. Pull it all the way round until it is almost touching the wire on the other side of the pliers.

Step 4 Snip the wire down, using your side cutters, and make a small loop at the end of the wire to finish.

Step 5 You should now have an s-shaped clasp.

Step 6 To use the s-shaped clasp, match it with a jumpring on either side. Close one of the sides completely and on the other side leave a small gap between the small loop and the center of the clasp to allow the connecting jumpring to pass through so you can attach and undo it.

MAKING A COIL

Coils can be used to add decoration to any piece, and they look especially attractive as spacers in between beads in a bead-and-wire design. They also form the first stage in making jumprings (see pages 36–37).

Step 1 Take a length of US 20 gauge (SWG 21, 0.8mm) wire. Place it in your round-nose pliers, right at the base of the jaws. Make sure there is no wire sticking out the back.

Step 2 Holding your pliers closed, use your hand to guide the wire around the back of the pliers to make a loop.

Step 3 When you can't go any further, open up your pliers and twist the wire around so that the tail of the wire is now facing the front.

Step 4 Clamp the pliers shut and guide the wire into making a second loop, directly below the one you have just made. Again, pull the wire around toward the back of the piece and when you can't go any further, release the pliers and move the whole piece back round to the front.

Step 5 Keep going in this manner, placing the new loop below the previous one each time to start to build up your coil. At first it seems a little tricky but once you have the hang of it you will speed up and it becomes a more natural movement. Often, the less you think about it and the quicker you go, the better they come out.

Step 6 Keep going to add more loops. As you add each one, make sure you are placing it at the bottom of the pliers. The jaws on the pliers are tapered so that they get thinner going up. To avoid a tapered look on your coil, place the wire at the base of the pliers each time.

Step 7 Once you are happy with the size of the coil you can take it off the pliers. Then either cut the end off to use it as a bead, or create a loop in the end to use it as a charm, or attach it to a piece of jewelry.

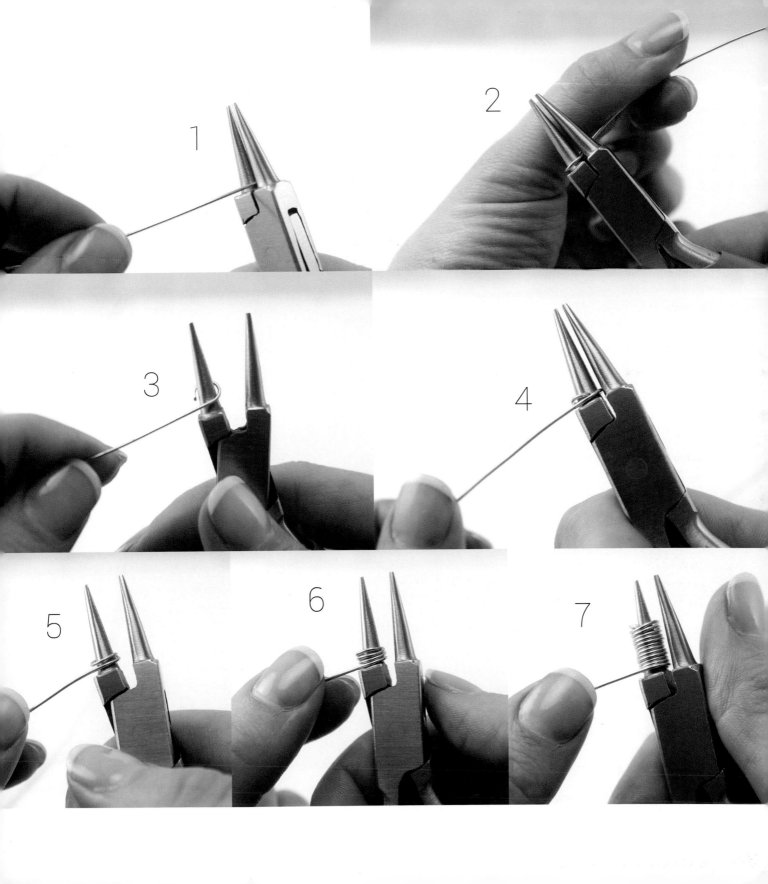

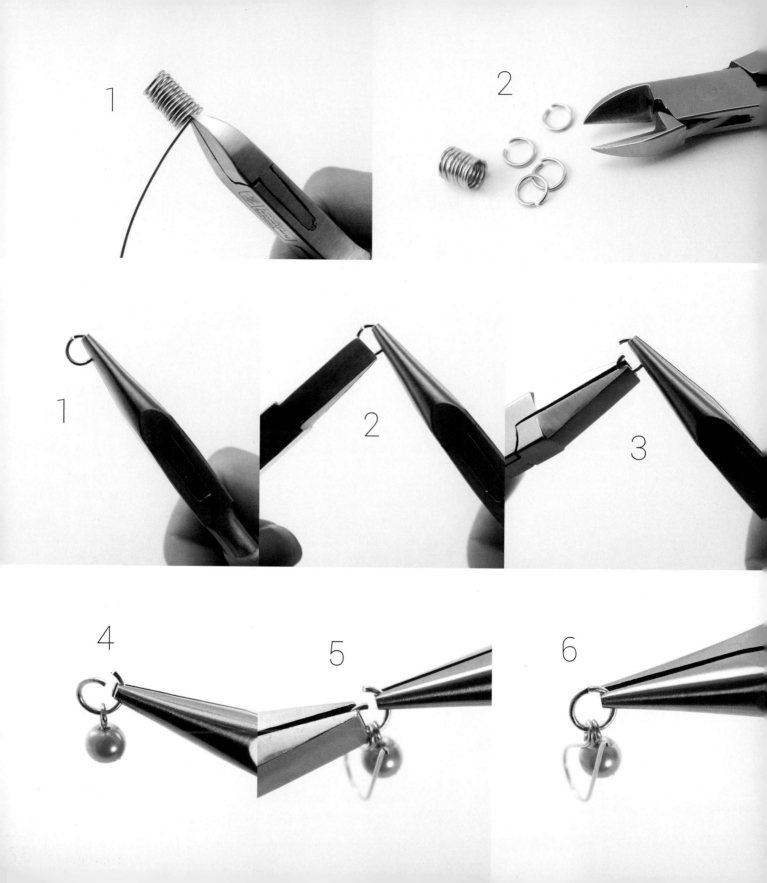

JUMPRINGS

Jumprings join pieces together and are therefore one of the most crucial components required in jewelry making. While you can buy them in all shapes and sizes, it is very handy to be able to make your own and is easy when you know how.

Making jumprings (top)

Step 1 Making a coil is the first stage to making jumprings. Refer to page 34 to make a coil. Once you have done so, you simply need to cut the wire. Use your side cutters to snip off the end of the wire, then cut in a straight line going up the coil, one loop at a time.

Step 2 As you cut, full circles with a split in the middle will drop off. These are your jumprings.

Opening and closing jumprings (bottom)

Jumprings are a vital component in most jewelry projects, so it is important to be able to open and close them properly. It will make the difference between your pieces staying together and potentially falling apart.

Step 1 Take your jumpring and place it in your chain-nose pliers so they are gripping one side with the split in the middle at the top.

Step 2 Use your flat-nose pliers (or another pair of chain-nose pliers) on the other side to grip the jumpring. From this stage onward it can be helpful to think of the pliers as extensions of your fingers.

Step 3 To open the jumpring, twist the two pairs of pliers in opposite directions so that one side of the jumpring goes back and the other goes forward. Never open a jumpring side to side—you always want to go from front to back so that you don't distort the circular shape of the piece.

Step 4 You are now ready to thread on anything you want to attach with your jumpring, such as a bead on a loop, a clasp, another jumpring, or a charm.

Step 5 To close the jumpring you need to use your chain-nose pliers on one side and flat-nose pliers on the other and bring your ring to a close. To close it securely you'll need to twist the jumpring backward and forward a couple of times using your pliers to move the two sides in opposite directions. You should hear the two sides of the wire clicking as they pass each other. Now bring them to a close in the middle. This "little wiggle" of the jumpring wire is to move the metal, making it tougher, and therefore giving a stronger join to the piece.

Step 6 You should now have a finished, perfectly closed ring. Do a last check to ensure there is no gap or light passing through the join.

USING HEADPINS

Headpins are short lengths of wire with one flat or shaped end that allow you to thread beads onto them without them falling off. They are very useful for seamlessly attaching beads to chain, threads, or other jewelry parts. Depending on the item you are making, there are two main ways to use headpins.

Looping headpins (top)

Step 1 Take a headpin with the flat or ball-end at the bottom.

Step 2 Thread on a bead then cut the wire down to ³⁄₈in (10mm) above the bead.

Step 3 Put the end of the wire into your round-nose pliers and twist the wire round to create a loop that meets the top of the bead. You can now use this to attach the bead to an earwire, bracelet, or necklaces.

Wire wrapping with headpins (bottom)

Step 1 Thread a bead onto your headpin then place your round-nose pliers slightly above the bead, near the top of the pliers.

Step 2 While holding the pliers shut with one hand, use your other hand to guide the wire up and over the plier jaw.

Step 3 Pull the wire behind the bead and across to the left. If adding the beads to chain, thread the chain onto the loop at this stage before wrapping.

Step 4 Now pull the wire forward and round, across the front of the bead, and continue wrapping in a clockwise direction around the top of the bead.

Step 5 After a few wraps you will start to see the gap between the loop and the top of the bead close, and your bead should be sat securely in place.

Step 6 Cut off any excess wire. The piece of jewelry should always be on the flat side of your cutters and the wire to be removed on the bevelled side.

Step 7 Use your chain-nose pliers to tuck in the sharp end of the wire to finish.

This bead can now be attached to pieces using a jumpring. Alternatively, if you were attaching this to a piece of chain, you would thread the chain onto the headpin at step 3, just below your pliers, and trap the chain in the loop at the top of the piece.

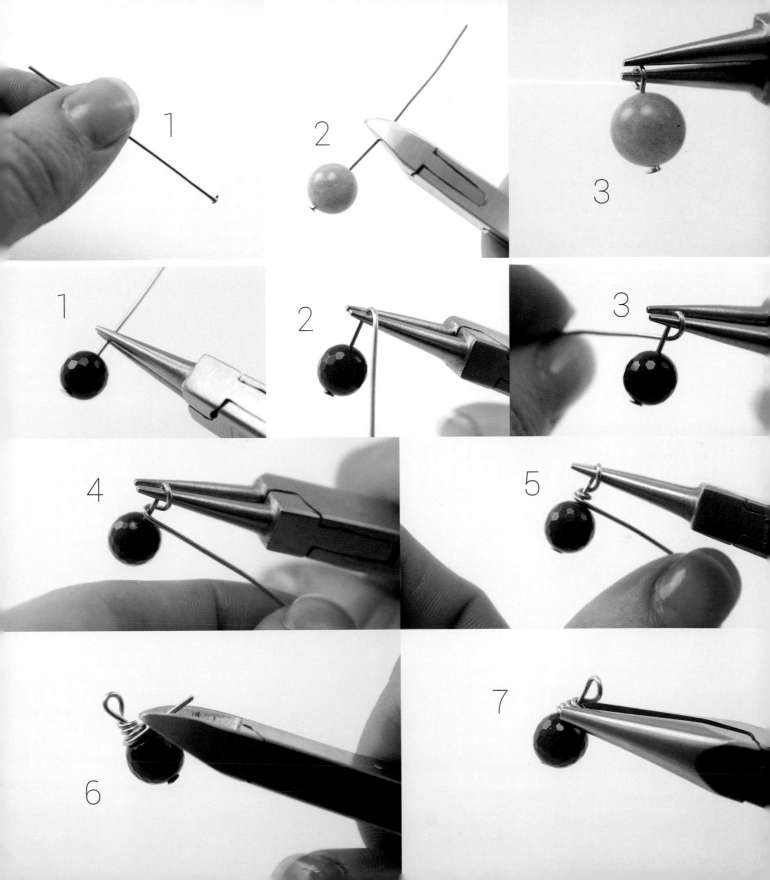

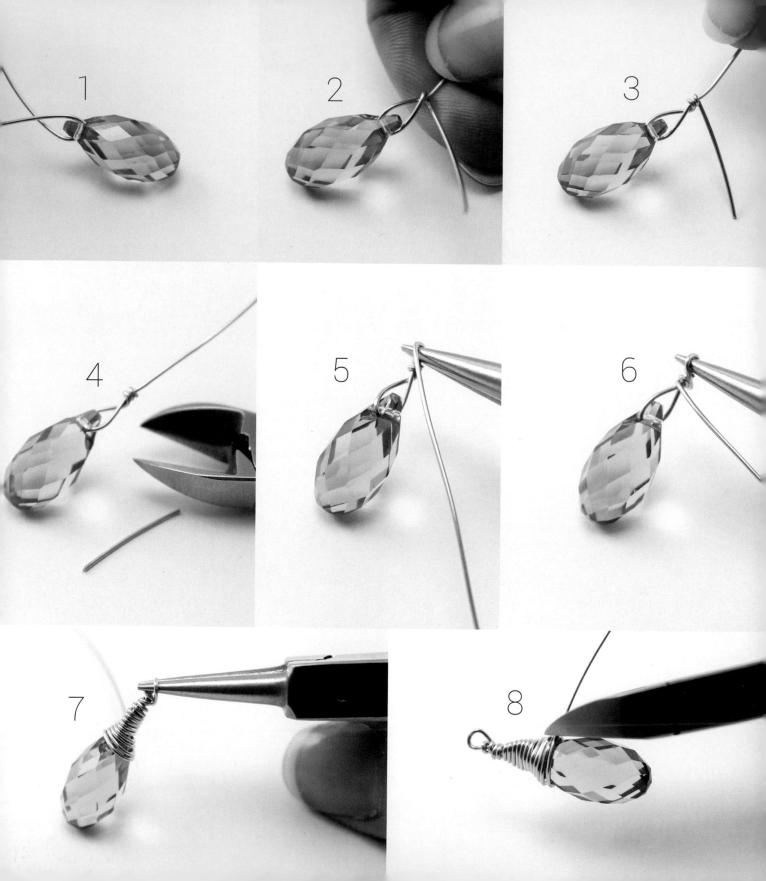

WRAPPING A BRIOLETTE

Briolettes are pear-shaped faceted gemstones or beads that look stunning in jewelry. They are top drilled, meaning they are often treated differently to regular center-drilled beads. Follow the steps below to learn how to wrap them for use in your projects.

Step 1 Thread the briolette onto a length of US 22 gauge (SWG 23, 0.6mm) or US 20 gauge (SWG 21, 0.8mm) thick wire, about 1¼in (30mm) down from the wire end. Cross the wires in the middle to make a loop where the bead sits.

Step 2 Take the short wire and twist it round the longer wire, making sure the wrap is centralized above the bead. If it isn't, use your fingers to adjust it at this stage.

Step 3 Do a couple of wraps here to secure the shorter wire to the longer one. Try to make the wraps nice and tight, placed neatly side by side with each other.

Step 4 Cut off any excess from the short wire and tuck the sharp end in using your chain-nose pliers.

Step 5 Next, place the long length of wire near the top of your round-nose pliers, just above the wire wrap created in the previous few steps. Pull the wire with your fingers up and over the top of the pliers to make a loop.

Step 6 Now wrap sideways around the wrap you originally created in circular motions, going down the piece toward the top of the bead.

Step 7 As you wrap, keep the wire as neat as you can with each layer placed just below the one before. Continue down until you cover the top of the bead, or for as along as you like, depending on how much wire you want to show.

Step 8 Cut off any excess wire and very gently tuck the sharp end in using your chain-nose pliers, being careful not to squash or damage the bead. Now you have a finished wrapped briolette ready to use.

MAKING SWIRLS

Wire swirls can add extra dimension as well as pattern to jewelry. Once you have mastered the basic technique you can use it to create all sizes of swirl and also experiment with different types of wire for varying effects. You can even use mini swirls to end-off spare strands of wire on wire-wrapped pieces.

Step 1 Take a length of US 20 gauge (SWG 21, 0.8mm) wire. Using your round-nose pliers, make a small loop at the end.

Step 2 Remove the loop from the pliers. There is no need to centralize the loop; it should be facing to one side like the number 9.

Step 3 Place the loop into your chain-nose pliers, making sure the tail of the wire starts just where the pliers end. (See the image for exact placing.)

Step 4 While holding your pliers in place with one hand, use your thumb to gently curve the tail of the wire around the original loop. Only go about a quarter of a circle round and then stop.

Step 5 Now shuffle your pliers round a bit so that once again the tail of the wire is just coming out of the end of the pliers. Hold that in place and gently curve the tail around the inner loop a bit more.

Step 6 You need to continue in this way, moving the wire a little way around the inside wire each time, then moving the pliers to catch-up with the wire. If you do too much at a time it can distort the curved shape of the wire, so you want lots of small movements.

Step 7 Keep curving the wire around itself, using the pliers to keep the piece flat, and build up the layers of your swirl until you are happy with the size of it. To finish off, take your chain-nose pliers to the end of the swirl and make a sharp bend in the wire at a 90-degree angle to give your swirl a stalk.

Step 8 You now have a completed swirl, which can be used to thread beads on to or attach to charm bracelets, etc. However, first you need to make a loop at the top so that it can easily be attached to your jewelry. To do this, cut off any excess wire, leaving approx $3/8$in (10mm) for the loop.

Step 9 Place the end of your wire in your round-nose pliers. Twist round to the side to make a loop.

Step 10 Centralize the loop using your pliers and fingers if needed.

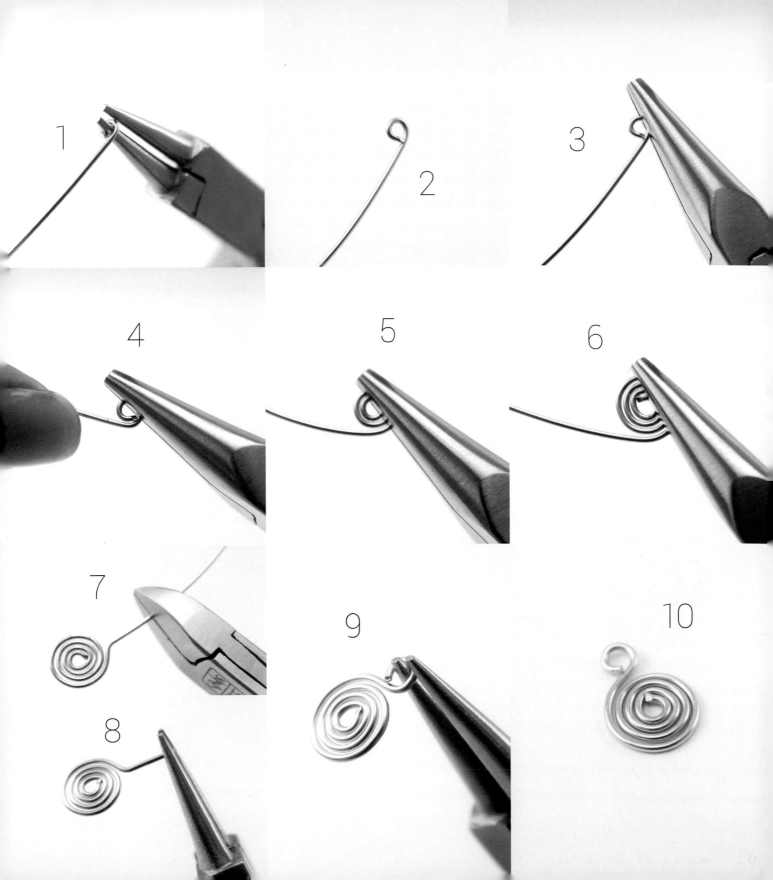

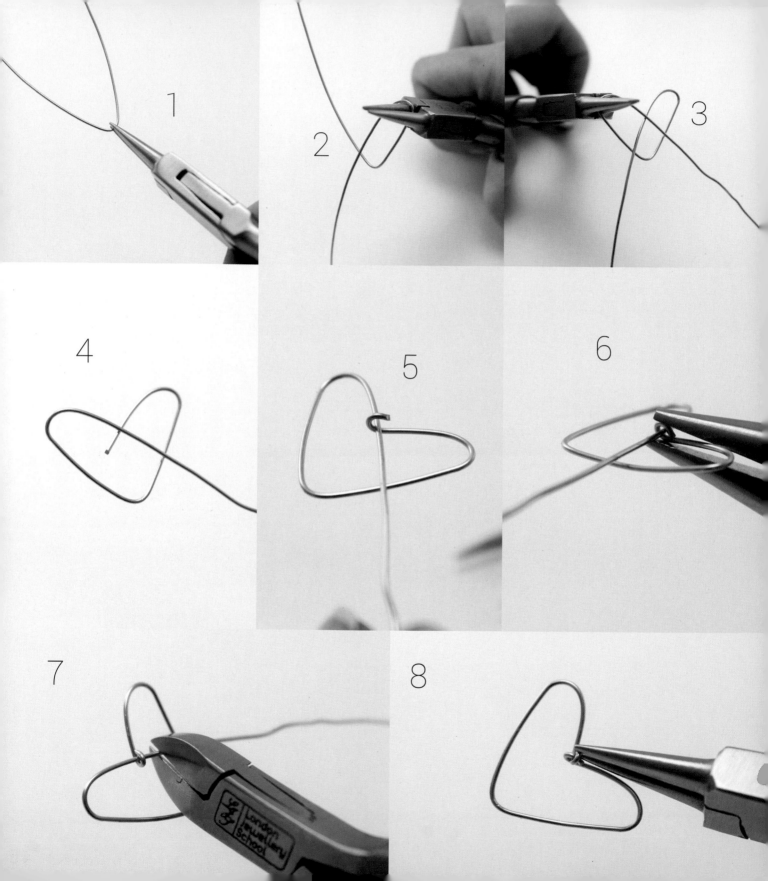

MAKING WIRE CHARMS

You can buy all manner of charms to incorporate in your jewelry but there is nothing better than being able to make your own. With a bit of wire and some pliers it is surprisingly simple to do just that. Follow the instructions below to make a heart, an infinity shape, and a bow-shaped charm to use in your collections.

Heart charm

Step 1 Take a length of US 20 gauge (SWG 21, 0.8mm) or US 18 gauge (SWG 19, 1mm) wire and make a soft V-shape in the wire using your round-nose pliers. This will form the point at the bottom of the heart.

Step 2 Place the left side of your wire into the bottom of your round-nose pliers, about $1^{3}/_{16}$in (30mm) up the wire and loop it over to the left, as shown in the image.

Step 3 Repeat the same on the other side of the wire to make the curved tops of your heart charm.

Step 4 Snip down the first bit of wire $^{3}/_{16}$in (5mm) away from where the two wires cross.

Step 5 Loop this piece over the wire coming from the left hand side.

Step 6 Create a half loop with your round-nose pliers and close the loop using your chain-nose pliers to make a snug and tight loop around the wire.

Step 7 Snip down the other side of wire, again $^{3}/_{16}$in (5mm) away from where the wires join.

Step 8 Use your round-nose pliers to create a loop back over the loop you made in step 6 and close this loop with your chain-nose pliers. You now have a completed wire heart charm that can be attached to earrings, necklaces, and bracelets using jumprings.

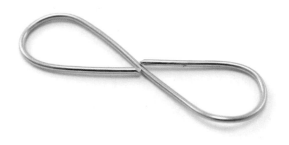

Infinity charm (top)

Step 1 Take a length of US 20 gauge (SWG 21, 0.8mm) or US 18 gauge (SWG 19, 1mm) wire and wrap it over a mandrel or a round pen or pencil until the wires cross at the front.

Step 2 Repeat on the other side so that you have two matching loops with the wires crossing in the middle.

Step 3 Snip down the excess wire where the wires meet.

Step 4 You may need to move the wires a little with your fingers to make a nice neat shape, and possibly even cut down some more wire if they are too long. Once you are happy with the shape, make sure the wire ends are placed so that they meet the middle of the piece. For extra strength, you can add a tiny drop of super glue where the wires join.

Bow charm (bottom)

Step 1 Take a length of US 20 gauge (SWG 21, 0.8mm) or US 18 gauge (SWG 19, 1mm) wire and wrap it around a mandrel or a round pen or pencil so that the wires cross at the front.

Step 2 Repeat the same on the other side, making sure you bring the wires up and over the pencil, and that the wire ends are sat next to each other or just crossing at the front.

Step 3 If they aren't already, gently cross the wires, making sure the wire from the first loop you made (on the right) is on top.

Step 4 Take that wire and push it under and to the back of the piece.

Step 5 Now guide it up and over to the front to create a full single wrap around the piece.

Step 6 Cut down the wires at the bottom of either side then file with a needle file to give a smooth finish. Flick the ends out using your round-nose pliers.

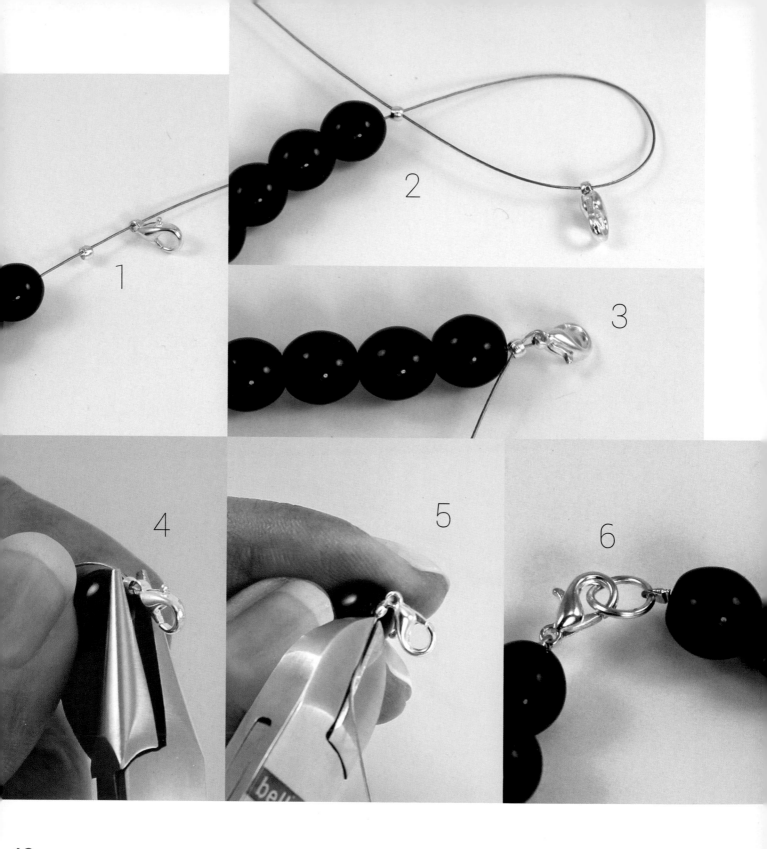

CRIMPING

Crimping is the technique of using tiny metal crimp beads to hold beading threads and findings in place. It is a fundamental technique used in making all types of beaded jewelry.

Step 1 Take a length of bead cord with your beads on, and thread it on a small crimp followed by a clasp.

Step 2 Thread the bead cord back through the crimp, but not through the clasp.

Step 3 Pull the bead cord tight to create a loop around the clasp with the crimp at the bottom. Pull it gently down until it sits on top of the beads.

Step 4 Using your chain-nose pliers, gently and firmly squash the crimp flat.

Step 5 Now you have squashed the crimp, it should hold everything in place. Cut off any excess cord with your side cutters.

Step 6 You have a finished crimped clasp. You can use the exact same technique for the other side of a length of beads, only this time replacing the clasp with a jumpring to match the other side, and will end up with a complete necklace or bracelet.

Statement NECKLACES

MOOD BOARD & DESIGN PROCESS

Gold wire has such a rich flavor to it. I really wanted to bring that out in this piece by combining it with fiery reds and orange colors. For my moodboard I have looked at different ways of combining these, taking inspiration from makeup, jewelry, and fashion. I have also looked at the different ways of building up layers in a piece using wire, chain, and beads, thinking about how to wrap the wire in a way that allows the colors of the beads to sit at the forefront.

CORAL GLOW

Wire necklace made with rich red and coral beads

This simple but effective wire-wrap design is a great way to show off a cluster of striking beads. Set against a thick hammered-gold chain, the rich red and coral tones will look stunning against a simple black top or dress.

TOOLS

- Chain-nose pliers
- Side cutters
- Round-nose pliers
- Bead mat (optional)

MATERIALS

- 15¾in (400mm) length of gold-plated, oval link, textured chain, 20 x 14mm link size
- 118in (3m) length of gold-plated wire, US 20 gauge (SWG 21, 0.8mm)
- 33 x pressed coral round beads, 12mm
- 27 x pressed glass red round beads, 10mm
- 2 x faceted drop, white mother-of-pearl beads, top drilled, 20 x 14mm
- 6in (15cm) length of gold-plated wire for clasp, US 18 gauge (SWG 19, 1mm)
- 12 x 7mm gold-plated jumprings

T|p *With any cluster piece it's best not to try to plan out exactly where each bead will go. Stick to the basic structure of the piece and techniques, then let the beads fall into place as you build up the front of the necklace. This will give more flow and movement to the piece.*

Step 1 Take the full length of gold-plated chain. Find the middle link and, using your fingers, wrap the end of a 98½in (2.5m) length of the 18-gauge gold-plated wire around it three times. Secure it tightly with chain-nose pliers as you go. Then, cut the starting end off and tuck in the sharp end to give a neat starting wrap.

Step 2 Thread two beads (one each of coral and red) on to the end of the wire. While holding the beads in place with one hand, wrap the wire back around the chain to attach them with the other hand. You want to wrap the wire twice around the chain, then you are ready to repeat the process with another two beads.

Step 3 With this cluster style of necklace it is best to have a slightly random approach to what beads to use where; each piece will be a little different depending on the beads and wire formation. Continue adding beads (two at a time) along the front of the chain to build up the first layer of beads. Wrap the wire around the chain twice between each set of beads.

Step 4 Once you have gone across five chain links in one direction, go back on yourself and add a second layer of beads. Keep adding them, two to three at a time, but with the second layer, instead of wrapping the wire around the chain, wrap it around the first layer of beads so that they sit below. Then add a third and fourth layer. The layers get a bit lost as you go along, but don't worry—that's the nature of a clustered piece.

Step 5 To build up the necklace, repeat the same steps on the other side (four more chain links, so that a total of nine chain links are wrapped with wire at the front of the necklace). As you build up the layers, you can add three or four beads at a time between wire wraps; you are aiming for a triangular shape. To finish, thread one white drop bead on the wire at the bottom of the piece, in the center.

6

7

Step 6 Position the white bead in the middle and wrap the wire back around the round coral bead above. Then take the wire and wrap it sideways around the gap between the coral bead and the white bead. Keep wrapping until the whole gap is filled and the top of the white bead is covered. Cut off the end of the wire and tuck or squash the wire end in using the chain-nose pliers.

Step 7 Check you are happy with the chain length and cut off any links that you don't need. Attach an s-shaped clasp (see instructions, page 33) on one side with a jumpring. On the other side, use the chain-nose pliers to attach a row of jumprings (using the technique on page 37). To complete your necklace, finish with a wire-wrapped white drop bead (see the "wrapping a briolette" instructions on page 41).

T i p *Look at the bigger picture—as you gradually build up the base of the piece, don't forget to look at the whole piece. Then add beads where they are needed to create the overall triangular shape.*

Variation

To create a matching pair of earrings, start by wrapping two of the white drop beads using the briolette wrapping technique (see page 41). Then add a large coral bead followed by a single chain link and a small red bead, using the basic technique for attaching beads using wire described on page 29. Finish with a handmade earwire (see page 30) or use a bought earwire finding.

T i p *Keep it tight. To make a long-lasting piece it's important to keep wrapping the wire to a previous section in between adding new beads. Try to make sure your wraps are nice and tight and go back over any loose bits with extra wraps of wire if needed.*

MOOD BOARD & DESIGN PROCESS

Taking the spring/summer season as inspiration I have looked at the combination of subtle greens and blues with an opaque white for this piece. It started when I saw these gorgeous green shoes and thought of putting them next to a rich deep blue that can be found in lapis beads and stones. It reminded me of the ocean and the way that waves shape stones to a rounded finish.

I then set about sourcing beads following on from this thought process. One of the great things about creating mood boards in this way is that it gives a story and continuity to your pieces or collections.

SEA BREEZE

Beautiful layered bead necklace in ocean tones

*This stunning necklace features a range of chunky stones in subtle greens and blues.
Simple bold designs are classic and the mix of faceted stones and irregular
pebble beads gives the piece a natural look.*

TOOLS

- Round-nose pliers
- Chain-nose pliers
- Side cutters
- Bead mat (optional)

MATERIALS

- 16 x white tumble pebble beads, sizes ranging from 20–30mm
- 14 x light green agate faceted beads, sizes ranging from 20–30mm
- 18 x blue lace agate round tumble beads, sizes range from 16–25mm
- 27 x periwinkle-blue faceted agate beads, sizes ranging from 8–20mm
- 18 x round lapis beads, 8mm, with large drilled center holes of 3mm or more
- 7 x 2in (50mm) silver-plated ball-ended headpins
- Approx. 120in (3m) length of Tigertail beading wire, 0.45mm thick
- 8 x silver-plated crimps, ⅛in (2mm)
- 1 x 13mm silver-plated oval closed jumpring, thickness: AWG 14 (1.5mm, SWG 16)
- Superglue (optional)

Step 1 Start by laying out the design and checking you have the correct components. Place your individual beads on a beading mat or work surface, starting with 14 white pebble beads, 12 green agate beads and 12 blue lace agate beads. These will make up the basis of your center three strands.

Step 2 Using the rest of the beads, lay out the full design on the beading mat. Place seven of the periwinkle agate beads in between the white pebble beads at the bottom of the necklace. Make sure you are happy with the design at this stage before you commit to threading.

Step 3 Take the seven periwinkle agate beads from the bottom of the necklace and thread each one on to its own headpin. Cut the headpin down to size and make a loop at the end of the bead using round-nose pliers (see page 38). You want all seven of them look like the bead in the picture.

Tip *As each of the beads are a different size, you may need to adjust the number of beads used in each section. Make sure the three strands at the base meet when held up as a necklace.*

Step 4 You are now ready to start threading the necklace. Cut three lengths of Tigertail wire, approx. 40in (1m) long each to allow plenty of room to work from. These three threads will make up the bottom half of your necklace. To start with you are only threading up to the first set of small round lapis beads. Thread your beads on to the strands as shown in the picture.

Step 5 When threading your beads on to the bottom strand, place the seven headpin beads (prepared in step 3) in between the white pebble beads at the center of the piece. Use the loop you created to thread the beads on to the Tigertail. Once you have threaded on all the beads, hold up the strands in front of a mirror to check they hang correctly.

Step 6 You now need to join all three strands together at each end of the necklace. Place the strands so the lapis beads sit in a diamond-like shape whereby the middle strand is pulled slightly back, allowing the beads at the end of the other two strands to meet above it. Thread all three strands through the fourth lapis bead so it sits at the top to complete the diamond shape. Repeat this on the other side.

Step 7 Before crimping above the beads to hold the bottom half of the necklace in place, hold the piece up and check that you are happy with how it sits. If needed, adjust the layout with your hands. Then place two ⅛in (2mm) silver-plated crimps over all three strands and squash them in place with the chain-nose pliers (see page 49). Repeat this on the opposite side. Once the crimps are secure, cut down two of the three Tigertail strands, leaving the center one to make the back of the necklace. To make it extra secure, you can put some superglue over the crimps at this stage. If you do, make sure you wait for it to dry before continuing.

Step 8 Now thread the rest of your beads on to each side of the piece and check you are happy with the final length.

Tip *Don't be scared to use a bit of superglue when needed. This necklace is very heavy and puts a lot of pressure on the crimps and findings over time. When applying glue, use a cocktail stick to get it into the gaps between the crimps and avoid getting any on your lovely beads.*

Step 9 To finish, attach the end of the Tigertail wire to the oval jumpring using two crimps with the standard crimping technique (see page 49) as shown in the image. Repeat this process on the other side to make a full necklace. Please note, there is no clasp on this piece as it is large enough to fit over your head. Again, you can apply a small amount of superglue over the crimps for extra security.

Tip *If you can't get the exact beads shown here, get creative. Experiment with different colors, shapes, and sizes. You will be amazed how many different necklaces you can make from the same pattern.*

MOOD BOARD & DESIGN PROCESS

For this piece I have taken a tropical, carnival-inspired theme and looked at the colors and styles typically on show. I have used the mood board to explore ways of adding feathers to outfits and jewelry, focusing on bright colors and combining that with the subtlety of chain.

I have also explored how feathers might sit on a chain by looking at other feather necklaces and thought about ways of adding beads and findings without damaging the delicate nature of the feathers. Now I am ready to make a truly tropical piece.

PARADISE

Tropical feather and chain neckpiece, bursting with color

Don't be afraid to give feathers a chance! Combine brightly colored feathers in a tropical theme with a selection of simple silver chains and chunky teal rock beads to create this funky, fashionable necklace. A summertime party piece that is truly unique.

TOOLS

- Chain-nose pliers x 2
- Round-nose pliers
- Side cutters
- Bead mat (optional)

MATERIALS

- Stripped coque feathers, 2–2^1/$_2$in (5–6cm): 7 x teal, 6 x navy, 6 x orange, 6 x pink, 6 x purple
- 31 x silver-plated foldover cord ends
- 5 x large teal faceted rock beads, 28mm x 24mm
- 16in (405mm) small silver-plated trace chain
- 16^1/$_2$in (420mm) medium curb chain, 5mm x 3mm link size
- 17^1/$_3$in (440mm) large curb chain, 8mm x 5mm link size
- 5 x 2in (50mm) silver-plated headpins
- 48 x 6mm silver-plated jumprings
- 1 x ^{3}/$_8$in (10mm) silver-plated lobster clasp

T|p *Feathers often have a natural curve or flow to them, so when making anything with feathers it's best to work with this and decide how best to fit this movement into your design. Position your feathers around the necklace in a way that you feel works visually.*

Step 1 Lay out all the feathers you will be using for this piece and allow a cord end for each feather. The feathers will have a long tail on them, which we will trim later. Attach a cord end to the base of each feather. To do this, first place the end over the feather, making sure the loop is facing away from the feather. Gently squash down one side using the chain-nose pliers. Once in place, squeeze down on it a second time to ensure it is secure.

Step 2 To complete the attachment, use the chain-nose pliers to squash down the other side of the cord end to make a simple, neat, and secure base for your feather. Finally, use the side cutters to clip off the long tail end of the feather as closely as you can to the end. Repeat this process with all of the feathers to prepare them for attaching to the chain.

Step 3 Once you have completed all the feathers (you should have six sets of five and an additional teal one, which we will use at the end), lay them out on a beading mat or work surface and finalize your design. I have used the teal rock beads with a set of five colored feathers in between each. It is a symmetrical design, starting in the middle and working outward: purple, pink, orange, navy, teal. I have also laid out my three silver-plated chains, large, medium, and then small at the top.

Step 4 Prepare the five teal beads for attaching to the necklace. Take a headpin and using round-nose pliers attach the beads to the headpin, creating a loop at the top (using the technique shown on page 38). Repeat this with all five beads.

Step 5 Now you are ready to start adding all the components to the chain. Take the large curb chain and start in the center. Using a jumpring, attach one looped bead to the middle link of the chain by threading the loop on the bead and the link of chain on to an open jumpring before closing it (see page 37). As always, make sure your rings are firmly closed and secure.

Step 6 Working outward from the center (one side to start with), attach your feathers using a jumpring for each. The first feather should be attached to the chain link directly next to the one you have just attached your bead to. At this stage check the direction of the feathers (feathers often have a curve or natural angle to them) and work with that to place it in the right direction to give a slight inward curve to the center of the piece.

Step 7 After attaching the first feather, continue adding them to each link along the chain, using your jumprings and chain-nose pliers to open and close them. After every five feathers, add a teal bead to complete the pattern.

Step 8 Complete one side of the necklace, from the center bead up to three sets of feathers and three beads. Then repeat the process, mirroring the feather layout on the other side, until all the feathers and beads are attached (excluding the additional teal feather).

Step 9 Now it's time to cut all three chains to the desired length (see page 66 for measurements). Hold the piece up to your neck in a mirror to check you are happy with the length of the chains before continuing. The chains are all slightly different lengths to give a layered effect to the piece, the largest chain being the longest at the bottom.

Step 10 Using two pairs of chain-nose pliers (or one pair of flat-nose and one pair of chain-nose pliers), attach all three chains together with a single jumpring on each side of the necklace.

Step 11 On one side, use an additional jumpring to attach your silver-plated lobster clasp. On the other side, create a chain of 10 jumprings by linking them together one by one. The jumpring chain gives the necklace an adjustable length feature. To complete the piece, attach the teal feather to the jumpring chain as a nice finishing touch.

Tip *Remember that each feather is unique and working with them is always better than trying to work against their natural direction.*

Tip *Consider how your necklace will hang—it looks a lot more clustered when worn than when spread out on a flat surface. Feathers have this effect on a design, so check you are happy with how the piece sits on your neck before creating the final piece, and keep this in mind when working with feathers in any project.*

MOOD BOARD & DESIGN PROCESS

I have taken inspiration from a range of sources including fashion trends, eye-catching beads, chain-based jewelry, a pink and brown color palette, and the layering effect used on lots of large statement necklaces.

For this piece I aimed to create a large statement necklace with a simple design. I took the chain as the main focus of the piece, first deciding on the style and length of this before adding the pink beads as embellishments.

When designing statement fashion jewelry, chain is an excellent staple that can help to bring volume and layers to a piece in a simple but effective way.

CHAIN ATTRACTION

Stunning pink and antiqued-copper chain necklace

Chain is always in fashion and to give it a more interesting vintage feel, here
I've used antiqued copper. Combined with pastel pinks and brassy pearls,
it makes a lovely chunky accessory for either day or eveningwear.

TOOLS

- Round-nose pliers
- Chain-nose pliers x 2
- Side cutters
- Bead mat (optional)

MATERIALS

- Selection of beads, for example:
  - 15 x large pink speckled oval beads
  - 26 x faceted pink acrylic beads, 8mm
  - 26 x 10mm brass Swarovski pearls
  - 15 x small round light-pink glass beads
- Antique copper ball-ended headpins
- 78¾in (2m) length of large link antiqued-copper chain
- 39⅜in (1m) length of medium link antiqued-copper chain
- 39⅜in (1m) length of small link antiqued-copper chain
- Antique copper jumprings, 7mm
- Large gold-plated clasp (or antiqued-copper clasp)

Step 1 Begin by attaching all the beads you are going to be using to headpins. Take a bead and place it on a headpin, ensuring that it doesn't fall off the end. Use side cutters to cut the wire down. You need to leave about ⅜in (10mm) of wire above the bead to make the loop with.

Step 2 Using either round-nose or chain-nose pliers, bend the wire at a 45-degree angle away from the center of the bead in preparation for making a loop with the wire. Make sure that you bend the wire from the top of the bead.

Step 3 Place the very end of the (bent) wire into the middle of your round-nose pliers and curve the wire round the pliers back toward the bead to make a loop. (For more detailed instructions, see page 38.)

Step 4 Repeat this process with all the beads. It is important to note that with the large beads, as the hole in them is large I have placed a small round light-pink bead at the bottom of the headpin to prevent it falling off.

Tip *Chain pieces are often fiddly because you have to juggle getting the lengths right with placing the beads correctly so it hangs well. Just take your time and make adjustments as you go.*

Step 5 Place the chains on a mat and play around with them until you are happy with the design. I have used three large-link chains, two medium and one small, a total of six chains. Once you have decided on the lengths, use two sets of chain-nose pliers held either side of a link of chain, and twist in opposite directions to open the link. Remove part of the chain to adjust to the desired length.

Step 6 Place the three lengths of the large link chain on your bead mat and check the lengths are correct. You need a long length that will be the bottom of your necklace, then a medium-length and a short-length piece. It can help to hold them up against you in front of a mirror to check. You will be adding a clasp, so allow about 4in (100mm) for that.

Step 7 Add the other chains to the mat and place the beads where you plan to attach them to check you are happy with the design. Place seven large oval beads on the bottom chain with a brass pearl and faceted pink bead in between each. Repeat the same design on the other two large-linked chain layers but using only five large oval beads on the middle chain and three on the top one. At this stage you are not attaching any beads, just placing them.

Step 8 To join the two smaller pink acrylic and pearl beads together in pairs, first open a jumpring using the two chain-nose pliers. Thread on the two beads then close the jumpring by wiggling the two sides shut with the pliers. Repeat with all the other pairs. (See page 37 for opening and closing jumprings.)

Tip *Mix it up! Remember that the project is just a guide and don't be afraid to try out different designs, use different colors, and experiment with different chain lengths and sizes. Take inspiration from your mood board and enjoy the design process along with the making.*

Step 9 Before attaching the beads to the chain, you need to join the chains together. Take six links off a spare piece of large-link chain and close each one of them. Then attach them together in a triangular shape as shown in the image, using jumprings. The top link will be used to attach a clasp to the piece and the bottom three links will be used to attach two each of the main chains. Create two of these triangle attachments (one for each side of the necklace). Attach the two triangle pieces to each side of the chains (without beads to begin with). This stage can take a little while as you need to add each chain individually, making sure that they are in the right order and tangle-free. Again, it is helpful to regularly hold the piece up in the air or in front of a mirror to check the chain lengths,

Step 10 Start by adding the bottom layer of beads. To add the large beads, thread them on to a jumpring, then thread the piece of chain you are attaching them onto through the same jumpring before closing it. Take care to ensure that all of your jumprings and loops are fully closed so that it is strong and secure.

Step 11 Once you have added all the large beads (I have placed them six links apart), add the pairs of smaller beads you prepared earlier. Open the jumpring on each and attach it to the chain in the middle of each large bead (on the third link). On the bottom chain I have added four extra pairs of small beads going up on each side, to add volume to the piece.

Step 12 When you hold your piece up, all the beads should hang in the right place; make adjustments or reposition them now if you need to. Once you are happy with the final design, you can add the clasp. Join a few links of the large chain to either end of the triangle attachments and attach a chunky gold-plated clasp in the middle.

MOOD BOARD & DESIGN PROCESS

I love sparkly jewelry and wanted to create a piece that not only sparkled but was literally covered in crystals.

To begin with I started looking at how crystals were used in furniture, around the house, and in clothes and jewelry. I then thought about a fresh color palette of combining pinks with brown and a touch of clear or white—something classy that would shine against a black dress.

These different elements came together to create the mood board that I then used to go bead and crystal shopping and designed the piece from there.

FORBIDDEN GLAMOUR

Silver chain-and-wire necklace with sparkling crystals

Diamonds may be a girl's best friend but crystals come a close second.
Using simple but effective techniques, you will first create the necklace "skeleton"
from silver chain before building up layers of crystals using silver headpins
and basic wire-wrapping techniques.

TOOLS

- Round-nose pliers
- Chain-nose pliers
- Side cutters
- Bead mat (optional)

MATERIALS

- 75in (1.95m) length of fine silver chain, flat oval style, 5 x 3.5mm link size
- 5 x 7mm large silver jumprings
- 200 x silver ball-ended headpins
- Swarovski wave pendant, champagne color, 42 x 22mm
- 23 x light pink faceted Czech crystal rondelles, 14 x 10mm
- 42 x white freshwater pearls, 10mm
- 48 x purple Swarovski bicones, 8mm
- 42 x pink freshwater pearls, 6mm
- 42 x gold metallic Swarovski bicones, 5mm
- 4 x 6mm medium silver jumprings
- Large silver leaf-shaped component, 11³/₁₆in x ⁷/₈in (45 x 22mm)
- 6in (15cm) length of silver wire to make clasp, US 18 gauge (SWG 19, 1mm), or bought clasp

Step 1 Cut three lengths of chain using the side cutters: short chain: 6¾in (170mm); medium chain: 10in (250mm); long chain: 11¾in (300mm). These will make up the front of your piece.

Step 2 Using two large silver jumprings, attach the large Swarovski pendant to one end of the longest length of chain. First attach one jumpring to the pendant then use a second jumpring to attach that to the chain (for how to close a jumpring, see page 37). This will be the focal end of this long-length necklace.

Step 3 Attach one of the pink crystal rondelle beads to the end of each of the other two lengths of chain cut in step 1. First thread the bead on to a silver ball-ended headpin and use your round-nose pliers to wrap the loop around the chain (see technique, page 38). You will be using this wire-wrapping technique throughout.

T|p *Master the techniques—there are a few specific techniques used in this piece and whether it works relies on getting those right, so before you start, practice with some oddments of chain and beads. Once you are confident, move on to the real deal. The main techniques used here are: wire wrapping with headpins (page 38), using jumprings (page 37), and creating a clasp (page 33).*

Step 4 Now add the first layer of crystals. Take the longest chain (with the large pendant on the end) and begin attaching the light pink rondelles to it using the wire-wrapping technique on ball-ended headpins described above. Each bead should be nine chain links apart on the opposite side of the chain.

Step 5 Once you have completed the longest chain, do the same with the other two. Again, make sure to attach each pink bead nine links above the previous one.

Step 6 Now you are ready to add the second layer of crystals and pearls. Take out eight silver headpins and a pair of each of the four other beads used in this piece, as pictured.

Step 7 Using the same wire-wrapping technique as before, attach each of the crystals and pearls, one by one, to the chain, in between the pink rondelles: white pearl, purple crystal, pink pearl, gold crystal (then repeat). This will give you eight beads, each one attached to a single chain link between the pink rondelles already attached.

Step 8 After completing your first set, work your way up the chain adding the same set of eight pieces in between each pink rondelle.

Step 9 To complete the bottom half of the piece, cover all three chains in this way and attach them together at the top with a single medium jumpring.

Step 10 See image for a close-up of the three chains joined at the top with a jumpring as described in step 9.

Step 11 Put your piece aside and cut three new lengths of chain to a length of 8¼in (210mm) each. Take the silver leaf-shaped component and, using one large and a medium silver jumpring, attach it to the three new lengths of chain. As always, make sure your jumprings are tightly closed.

Step 12 On the other side of the leaf-shaped component, use another large and a medium silver jumpring to attach the rest of your piece. You should end up with three crystal-covered chains, followed by the leaf-shaped component, then the other three lengths of chain.

Tip *This piece, while not that difficult technically, is not for the faint-hearted. It takes a day or so to make, as attaching all of the marvelous pearls and crystals is a lengthy process. It is best to make this piece over a number of evenings or days doing bits and coming back to it. Be patient, it's worth it!*

Step 13 To attach a clasp to the end of the chain, join the three pieces together using a medium jumpring and attach a clasp at the same time. I used a handmade silver hook clasp, made using 18-gauge silver wire (see techniques on page 33). You can also use a bought clasp or finding.

Step 14 Now to add the final chain to your piece. Cut three lengths of 6³/₁₆in (155mm) chain and attach them to the first jumpring at the end of your crystal covered chain section. This will be on the opposite side of the piece from where the leaf-shaped component sits.

Step 15 Add a large jumpring to the end of these three new pieces of chain to attach them together and hook in your clasp to see the complete chain-based top end of the necklace.

Step 16 As a finishing touch, attach a row of the purple crystals to the length of chain on the opposite side of the leaf-shaped component and a single one to the jumpring at the top of the component. Just for some added sparkle.

Tip *The lengths of chain given in the steps are a great guide but everyone has a different shaped neck and prefers different lengths for their necklaces. Hold up the piece against yourself (or the person you are making it for) in a mirror and check you are happy with where the chain is sitting before committing.*

Designer EARRINGS

MOOD BOARD & DESIGN PROCESS

Feathers remind me of festivals and beachwear so for my mood board I have looked at these areas, exploring rich blue and white hues mixed with gold, silver, and browns.

I have taken inspiration from the "dream catcher," looking at how they use feathers dangling off a circular shape, and used a similar structure for my earrings to ensure the feathers have space to hang and are able to create the most impact.

I have chosen strong blue patterned feathers as the main feature of the piece and combined these with subtle round beads to complement the overall look.

FIESTA

Simple show-stopping feather earrings

Feathers have long been used in jewelry design to give an animalistic and funky flair to pieces. In this project, learn to make an effective pair of designer earrings using striking blue feathers and matching beads to create catwalk worthy designs.

TOOLS
- Round-nose pliers
- Chain-nose pliers x 2
- Side cutters or scissors
- Bead mat (optional)

MATERIALS
- 10 x dyed blue feathers (in a mixture of sizes approx. 40–100mm/1⁹/₁₆–4in)
- 10 x silver-plated cord ends
- 12 x 4mm silver-plated jumprings
- Selection of cream and blue beads
- Clear nylon beading thread
- 2 x 6mm closed silver-plated jumprings
- 2 x silver-plated crimps, medium-sized, 2 x 2mm
- 2 x silver-plated earwires, handmade (see page 30) or bought

Step 1 Take the end of one or the feathers and place it in the middle of a cord end. If your feathers have strands going all the way to the top of the stalk, you may need to pull off a little bit at the top to make room for the cord end, or you can just crimp over the strands.

Step 2 Using the chain-nose pliers, gently and firmly push one side of the cord end over the top of the feather stalk to hold it in place. Be sure to push down quite hard to hold the feather securely. This bit can be fiddly but it gets easier with practice.

Step 3 Next, fold the second side of the cord end over, on top of the initial fold, to complete the crimping process. Again, push down firmly with the chain-nose pliers to secure the feather in place. You should not be able to pull the feather out of the crimp after this stage. If you can, repeat with a new cord end and try making firmer folds.

Step 4 Repeat stages 1–3 on each of your 10 feathers. I have used five on each side: one long one for the center of the earring, two medium-length ones, and two shorter ones. Try and make sure the lengths match by laying out your design on a beading mat before starting. You then need to add a 4mm jumpring to each feather by threading one through the loop and closing them with your chain-nose pliers.

Step 5 Once all of your feathers are attached to a closed jumpring via a cord end, you can begin stringing your earring. Take a long length of nylon thread (approx. 20in/500mm gives plenty of room to work) and thread on your five feathers in order, with a round cream-colored bead in between each feather.

Tip *I always lay out my designs on my bead mat before I start, checking that I like how they look and ensuring I have everything I need to make the piece. In particular, check the size and order of the feathers and beads for your arrangement.*

Step 6 When all your feathers are in place for both earrings, with cream-colored beads in between, you can add the remainder of your beads in any pattern you like. I have chosen two different-sized blue beads, another white bead, and then a final three blue beads. Hold your earrings up at this stage and check how the feathers hang before moving on to the next stage.

Step 7 We now need to crimp the earring in place. Take the two ends of your nylon cord and place a silver-plated crimp over them both, followed by a 6mm closed jumpring. Push the jumpring and crimp down towards the beads, your earring will start to take an oval/teardrop shape.

Tip *As always, ensure that your crimps are tightly closed and that there are no gaps in your jumprings. This will make for a secure and long-lasting piece.*

Step 8 To hold this all in place you need to thread both ends of the nylon cord back through the crimp (not through the jumpring)—this encases the jumpring in a loop made from the nylon cord (for full details on basic crimping, see page 49). Pull the piece tight so that the crimp is now at the top of the beads and the jumpring is securely captured in the thread. You then need to squeeze the crimp closed with chain-nose pliers and cut off any excess thread with side cutters or a small pair of scissors.

Step 9 Make sure you repeat this crimping process with both earrings and then you just need to add the earwires to finish. Using your chain-nose pliers, open up a 4mm jumpring. Use this to attach the top of your earrings to the loop at the base of your earwire. Use the pliers to tightly close the jumpring to finish.

Tip *When wearing or selling a piece like this, remember that they are feathers and can be damaged if not taken care of.*

MOOD BOARD & DESIGN PROCESS

For this piece I wanted to combine two time-defying classics: pearls and a nautical theme. I began by looking through fashion magazines for stripy navy and white designs and sailor-style clothes. I then thought about the colors that freshwater pearls often come in, such as whites, golds, and navy. At the end of the designing phase I got all my pearls out on a bead mat and played around with different wires and chains until I was happy with the look and feel.

From this mood board and basic techniques, a whole collection could be made.

PEARL LUSTER

Elegant navy and bronze pearl drop earrings

Pearls look lovely at the end of a little chain and the combination of navy, cream, brass, and gold tones make this a truly versatile set. They work equally well worn with a striped blue and white top or a simple evening dress. If you like pearls, this is a perfect beginners' project.

• Round-nose pliers
• Chain-nose pliers
• Side-cutters
• Bead mat (optional)

MATERIALS
• 4in (100mm) of thin gold-plated chain
• 20 x small gold-plated round beads, 2mm
• 2 x peachy gold Swarovski pearls, 12mm
• 20 x gold-plated headpins
• 6 x cream-colored freshwater pearls, 6mm
• 6 x iridescent navy freshwater pearls, 5mm
• 6 x brass-colored freshwater pearls, 4mm
• 6in (150mm) gold-plated wire, US 20 gauge (SWG 21, 0.8mm)
• Pair of earwires, handmade (see page 30) or bought

Step 1 Cut the gold-plated chain in half to form two 2in (5cm) lengths. Put a small gold bead followed by a large peachy gold pearl on to a headpin and wrap it around the end of one piece of chain. (For wrapping techniques, see page 38.)

Step 2 Next, attach one each of the three different types of pearl you are using: a cream one on the first link, navy on the second link, and peachy gold on the third. Each time, use the same basic wire-wrapping technique with your round-nose pliers. Make sure you thread a small, round, gold bead on to the headpin before each pearl to give a ball-ended look.

Step 3 Add two more sets like this, going one link up the chain each time until you have a complete cluster of 10 pearls in total (including the large center pearl at the bottom).

Step 4 Set the piece you are making aside and create a matching pair of swirls with loops on the end using your pliers (see page 42 for instructions to make swirls). You want the swirls to mirror each other in order to make the earrings symmetrical.

Step 5 Using the loop, join one swirl on to the opposite end of the chain to where the pearls sit.

Step 6 To finish, attach an earwire to the loop at the end of the spiral and your earring is complete. Repeat the same process to make a second earring using the matching spiral you made in step 4.

Tip *Vary the length of chain you use to create different styles with these earrings. You could make them without any chain gap, a very small amount, or even longer for a slightly different finished piece.*

1

2

3

4

5

6

MOOD BOARD & DESIGN PROCESS

Many people shy away from using colors like orange
and yellow, but in this piece I decided to throw them all
in together. For my mood board I wanted to focus the
design around springtime, bright and fresh colors, and
create a palette of oranges, pinks, yellow, and gold.

I looked at gemstones, flowers, and even cakes
for ideas and came up with a chandelier-style pair of
statement earrings. I also went out and bought some
cakes as the pictures looked so good!

SPRING BURST

Luxurious pair of vibrantly colored chandelier earrings

This design involves a spring-inspired color palette along with chain and wire to create
a diamond-structured top and a beady dropped base. Once you've mastered the basics,
the colors can be adapted to suit any time of year.

TOOLS

- Round-nose pliers
- Chain-nose pliers
- Side cutters
- Flat-nose pliers
- Beading mat (optional)

MATERIALS

- 78in (2m) gold-plated wire US 22 gauge (SWG 23, 0.6mm)
- 2 x Swarovski orange faceted briolette beads, 16mm
- 4 x yellow faceted round beads, 6mm
- 10 x light pink round faceted beads, 8mm
- 4 x fushia pink round faceted beads, 8mm
- 4 x faux pearl round beads, 8mm
- 24 x round peach beads, 4mm
- 24 x round pink beads, 4mm
- 16 x gold-plated headpins
- 6⁵⁄₁₆in (160mm) length of thin gold-plated chain
- 2 x 5mm gold-plated jumprings
- Pair of gold-plated earwires, handmade (see page 30) or bought

Tip *Vary the look—try different colors, less rows for a simpler piece or leaving the middle wire curved for a triangle (and not diamond) finish.*

Step 1 Start by wrapping the two briolettes, one for each earring. Take the end of some 22-gauge wire and thread it through the bead. After an inch (25mm) or so, bend the wire and cross it over as shown in the image.

Step 2 Wrap the briolette (for instructions on how to wrap, see page 41). When you have come to the end of the wrap leave 1³⁄₁₆in (30mm) spare and cut it off the wire spool. Then create a mini loop at the end of the wire using chain-nose pliers, ready to create a swirl.

Step 3 Use your chain-nose pliers to curl the wire around the loop and make a finished swirl that sits at the end of the briolette wrap (for how to make swirls, see page 42). Repeat on the other bead so that you have a matching pair.

Step 4 Take the 22-gauge wire and make a centered loop at one end. Leave a small gap and thread on the briolette before fully closing the loop.

Step 5 Thread on one of the yellow faceted beads and cut the wire approximately ³⁄₈in (10mm) above where the bead sits, in preparation to make a loop.

Step 6 Make a loop using the chain-nose pliers (see page 26). Try to make your loops a consistent size; this can take a bit of time and comes with practice.

Step 7 Repeat steps 4–6 with a light pink faceted bead and then another yellow bead to start building up a beady chain (using wire loops) that will form the center of your earring.

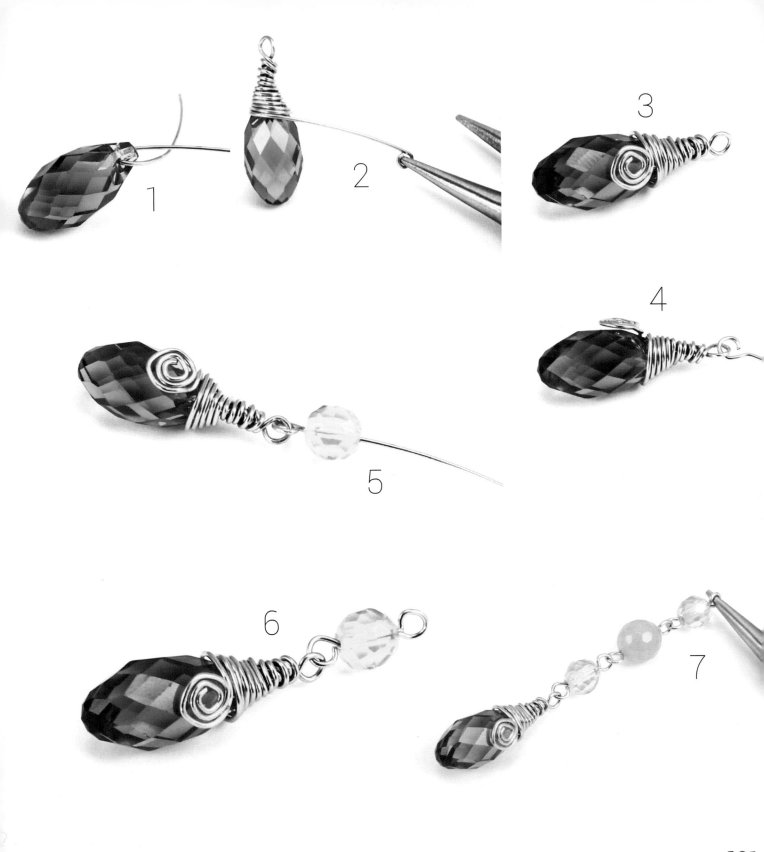

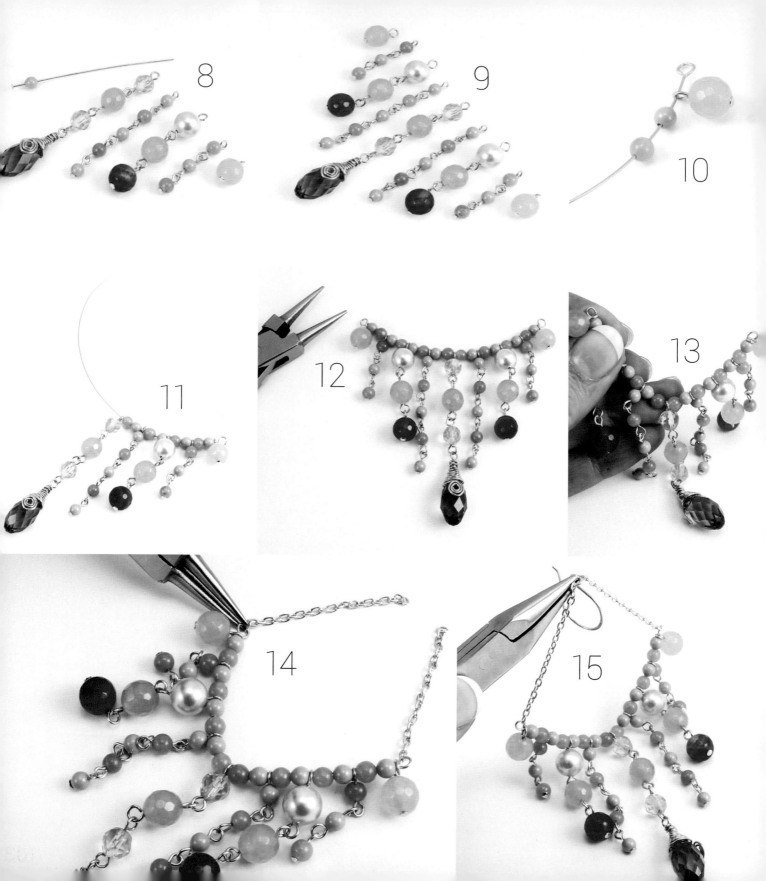

Step 8 Using a headpin, thread on a round peach bead and loop the end. Then use the process in steps 4–6 to add the other beads in sequence going up to make the second row of beads. Copy the pattern of beads shown in the image to make one full side of an earring. You should have five full rows in total that vary in lengths from one to five beads.

Step 9 Do the same for the other side so that you have a full set of nine dangly bead lengths. Then repeat to make the other earring.

Step 10 Take a 6in (150mm) length of the 22-gauge wire and make a full loop at the end. You are going to use this to thread on the bead strands you have just made. Start by adding the first single light pink bead on a headpin followed by a round peach bead and round pink bead.

Step 11 Following the two small beads, thread on the second row of three dangly beads. Continue to add each row you have created in order, with a set of one small peach bead and one small pink bead in between each row.

Step 12 Once you reach the center be sure to mirror the pattern on the other side, which means changing the order of the two small beads separating each row. When you come to the end, cut the wire down and make a loop using the round-nose pliers to secure everything in place.

Step 13 Using your hands, gently bend the wire so that the middle forms a point at the bottom, creating a V-shape. Do this to both earrings at the same time to get a matching bend.

Step 14 Attach a 1³⁄₈in (40mm) length of chain to each end of the earring using the loops you made in step 12.

Step 15 To finish, use a small jumpring to join together the two lengths of chain and an earwire.

T|p *Always make sure your loops are completely closed to avoid any beads falling off at a later date.*

T|p *There are lots of different lengths in this piece, so to make it match try to keep your loops and wires of a similar size, it's a good idea to practice on some oddments of wire before starting.*

MOOD BOARD & DESIGN PROCESS

This piece began when I came across some stunning amethyst briolette stones. I wanted to find a way to show them off so I used a mood board to see how deep purple could be combined with a bright turquoise to accentuate its color. I then looked at how this related to other areas of fashion and jewelry, even drinks. The color combination reminded me of fruity cocktails.

After creating the board I settled on a large hoop design. When creating your mood boards don't forget to look beyond jewelry and fashion for inspiration; look also at interiors, scenes, and landscapes.

PURPLE HAZE

Crystal-covered super-sized hoop earrings

*In this fun project, you'll make a gorgeous pair of sparkling hoops and at the same time
learn a great set of techniques you can adapt to create a range of stunning looks.
Start by making a simple circular frame and find out how to attach your crystals
using a basic wire-wrapping technique.*

TOOLS

- Round-nose pliers
- Chain-nose pliers
- Side cutters
- Bead mat (optional)
- Mug, cup, or glass for shaping wire around
- Wooden mandrel (or other object such as a glue stick, for shaping wire)

MATERIALS

- 39in (1m) silver-plated wire, US 18 gauge (SWG 19, 1mm)
- 2 x 5mm silver-plated jumprings
- 152in (4m) silver-plated wire, US 26 gauge (SWG 27, 0.4mm)
- 47 x turquoise-colored button beads, 4mm
- 16 x amethyst briolettes, range of sizes from 8–12mm in length
- 2 x Swarovski crystal teardrop faceted pendants, 18mm
- 2 x silver-plated earwires, handmade (see page 30) or bought

Tip *The key to making this, and many wire-wrapped pieces, is to keep wraps tight and neat. This can take a bit of practice but it's easy once you get the knack. If the amount of wraps you are doing doesn't feel like enough, do more. A tightly wrapped piece will last longer and sit better.*

Step 1 Make the largest wire hoop first. Take the 18-gauge silver plated wire and shape with your hands around a mug, cup, or glass to give it a circular shape. Wrap it around 1½–2 times.

Step 2 Take the curved wire off the cup and use your hands to finish shaping until you are happy with the size of the circle. Use the side cutters to cut off the excess wire until you have a round piece that is slightly bigger than your finished design. The length of the cut wire should be approximately 6in (150mm). Repeat steps 1–2 to make a pair.

Step 3 Make a loop in the wire at either end using round-nose pliers; this will be the top of your hoops. (To recap on how to make perfect loops, see page 26.) With each stage of this project, remember to repeat each process to make a pair.

Step 4 To complete the circle, join the two loops together with a jumpring. Use the chain-nose and flat-nose pliers to close the jumpring and make sure it is securely closed (for tips on closing jumprings, see page 37).

Step 5 Cut a length of approximately 60in (1.5m) of 26-gauge silver-plated wire to attach to the base of the hoop. Wrap it around the right side of the hoop with your fingers, keeping each wrap as close and neat as possible. To secure the end after the first few wraps, cut the wire end off and tuck in the sharp bit with the chain-nose pliers. Keep the long end of wire, as this is what you will secure your beads to.

Step 6 Work your way around nearly a quarter of the hoop base with the wire wrapping, then start to thread on the beads. Attach each bead on one by one, wrapping the wire around the base twice in between each bead. Use a total of five of the small turquoise beads at this stage.

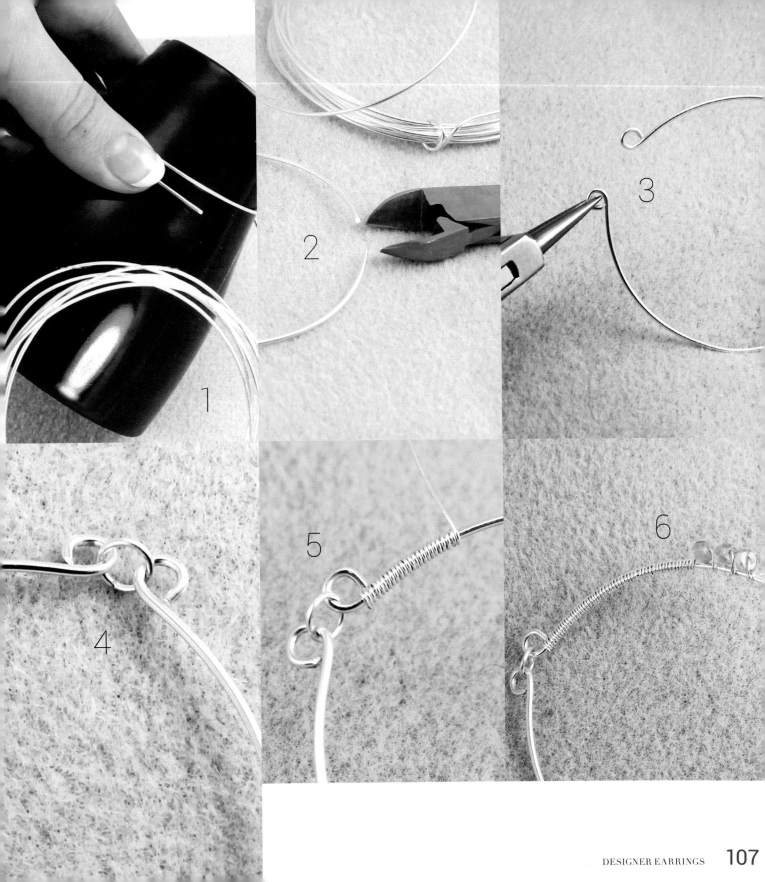

Step 7 Attach three of the amethyst briolettes, using a smaller one either side of a large briolette. Wrap the wire three times around the base between each one. To make sure your earrings match and are symmetrical you need four sets of these briolette trios approximately the same in size.

Step 8 Add three more of the small turquoise beads followed by a briolette before adding the main center bead. Attach the clear Swarovski crystal teardrop using a few wraps of wire either side. Make sure that it is central in the hoop and sits flat after the briolettes.

Step 9 Continue round and mirror the design on the second half of the earring. If you run out of wire at any stage, tuck the end in with the chain-nose pliers and wrap a new piece of wire where the last one ended. Just make sure to overlap the wires a little so that it all stays in place.

Step 10 Take the 18-gauge wire and wrap it around the wooden mandrel at the largest end (or you can use a glue stick) to create a curved shape about 4in (100mm) in length.

Step 11 Pull the wire out a bit to give a slightly larger oval shape and cut the wire down using side cutters. Repeat the process to make a matching pair.

Tip *As always with earrings, it's best to make the pair at the same time. That way all the measurements are right and you will be sure to have a matching pair.*

Step 12 Attach the oval wire shape you have just made to the outer hoop at one end by wrapping around some 26-gauge wire several times. You will need about 20in (500mm). Cut and tuck the end in when it is securely attached.

Step 13 Repeat the same process on the other side with another 20in (500mm) length of wire.

Step 14 After you have matched the wire wrap on the other side, don't cut the finishing end off but thread a row of the small turquoise beads on and wrap it over the other side of the hoop to hold everything in place.

Step 15 Finally, attach an earwire to the top of your hoop using the silver-plated jumpring.

Tip *These earrings are quite heavy. They are at the larger end of what can work well as earrings and using stones much heavier than the ones used is not recommended. If in doubt, experiment. You can always cut it off and start again.*

Couture
BRACELETS

MOOD BOARD & DESIGN PROCESS

Before creating this mood board I had bought some silver spiked charms from a bead shop, so I used that as the starting point. I looked at biker-chick fashion and saw that there was a trend for combining strong metallic shapes with soft, feminine colours. This gave me the idea for using pink to off-set the edginess of the spikes and I created my board and overall piece from there.

I particularly liked the spiked collar and thought of creating a pink one in a similar style—there's an idea for another piece!

LOVE HURTS

Feminine but edgy piece on a silver curb chain

Release your inner biker chick with this spiky pink chain. Follow the steps to attach
cast charms before adding a touch of flair with some pretty faceted beads.
Once you have mastered the basic technique, it can easily be applied to make
a matching necklace, earrings, or even a ring for your own bespoke set.

TOOLS

- Round-nose pliers
- Chain-nose pliers
- Flat-nose pliers
- Side cutters
- Beading mat (optional)

MATERIALS

- 7in (180mm) silver-plated curb chain, 8 x 5mm link size
- 15 x silver-plated spike charms, 13/8in (35mm) long
- 38 x silver-plated jumprings, 7mm
- 1 x silver-plated jumpring, 12mm
- 1 x 9/16in (14mm) silver-plated large bolt ring clasp
- 22 x pastel pink faceted rondelle beads, 5mm
- 22 x clear red faceted rondelle beads, 5mm
- 22 x silver-plated headpins

Tip *Get the spacing right on your headpins. Make sure that you cut down the headpins at the right point, approximately 3/8in (10mm) from the top of the bead and make a round loop that meets the bead. Avoid any gaps in between the bead and loop for a professional finish.*

Step 1 Take a length of curb chain that is big enough to fit around your wrist and attach five spiked charms to the center chain link using three separate 7mm jumprings; the middle one is on its own jumpring with the two either side of the center charm sharing one.

Step 2 Count six links round either side of the center link (or a quarter of the way round the whole chain) and repeat the process, adding another five charms either side. You should be left with three spike clusters that are equally separated around the chain.

Step 3 Attach the large jumpring to one end of the chain and the large bolt ring clasp to the other end, using a smaller jumpring to join it.

Step 4 Set chain aside and thread a pink bead followed by a clear red bead on to a headpin and make a loop at the top. Repeat this to make 22 sets of beads. (For instructions on using headpins, see page 38.)

Step 5 Using a small jumpring, attach one bead set to each chain link starting from the center spike cluster out to the side ones.

Step 6 You should now have five bead sets on each side of the middle spikes. (Note: if you are making a larger bracelet you will have more links between the spikes so you will need more bead sets to fill the spaces.)

Step 7 To finish, carry on adding the bead sets all the way up to the clasp, one on each chain link, which is a total of six on each side.

MOOD BOARD & DESIGN PROCESS

There is nothing more exciting than a stash of gemstones. I knew I wanted to create a piece that allowed the stones that I had chosen to stand out, so I began the mood board by looking at other pieces of jewelry that used stones as a central part of the design. I then looked at colors and saw that combining pinks with blues and grey gave a lovely finish, both against gold and silver. It all felt quite summery and beach-like so I finished my board with some textures and a simple white dress that would help to let the stones do the talking.

BEACH BABE

Semiprecious stones take center stage

Combine semiprecious stone nuggets with silver wire to make this colorful arm candy.
After creating a silver wire base, learn to wrap the nuggets around the bangle to show
off some stunning stones in this beachcomber-inspired, chunky piece.

TOOLS

- Round-nose pliers
- Chain-nose pliers
- Side cutters
- Mug, cup, or glass
(for shaping metal)
- Beading mat (optional)

MATERIALS

- 39in (1m) length of silver-plated wire, US 18 gauge (SWG 19, 1mm)
- 78in (2m) length of silver-plated wire, US gauge 20 (SWG 21, 0.8mm)
- 5 x turquoise nuggets, 20mm
- 5 x labradorite round beads, 10mm
- 5 x rose quartz round faceted beads, 15mm
- 5 x amethyst nuggets, 15mm

Step 1 Take a length of 18-gauge wire and wrap it two or three times around a cup or mug to give it a circular shape.

Step 2 Place the wire on your wrist, wrapping it round several times, to get the correct bangle size and making sure you can take it off. Wrap one end of the wire around the others two or three times to secure it in place. Try to make the wraps as close together and neat as possible.

Step 3 Once you have tightly wrapped the wire, cut off the end and squash the sharp bit into the wires using your chain-nose pliers. You should be able to run your finger over it and not feel anything sharp. If you can, give it another push with the pliers until fully tucked in.

Step 4 Repeat the same wire-wrapping process approximately two-thirds of the way around the bangle with the other end, to secure the base of the piece in place. Next, take a long length of gauge-20 wire (as long as you can manage, 40–75in/1–2m) and wrap it 5–6 times around one of the wraps you have just made in step 2 or 3. This is to firmly attach it to the piece before threading on your beads.

Step 5 Thread on your first stone, a turquoise nugget. Leave a small gap in the wire between the stone and the bangle and arrange the stone so that it sits flush on the bangle base.

Step 6 Bend the wire down and using your fingers place the bead in the correct place ready to be attached with wire wrapping.

T i p *You don't have to stick with silver wire—try this piece in gold, copper, or colored wires. Just be sure to use the correct thickness so that it is durable.*

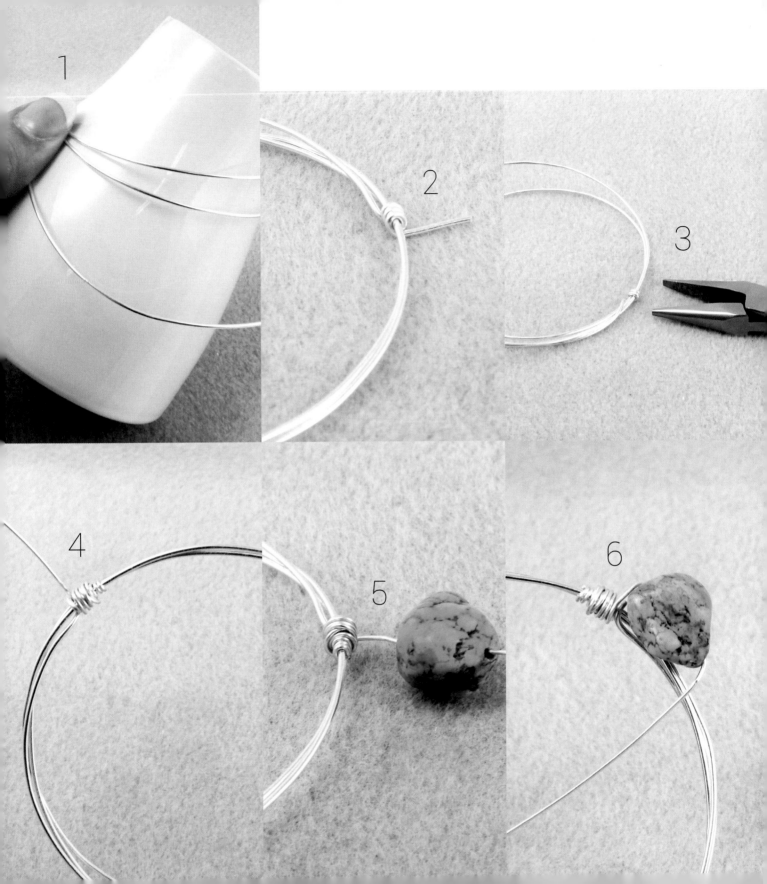

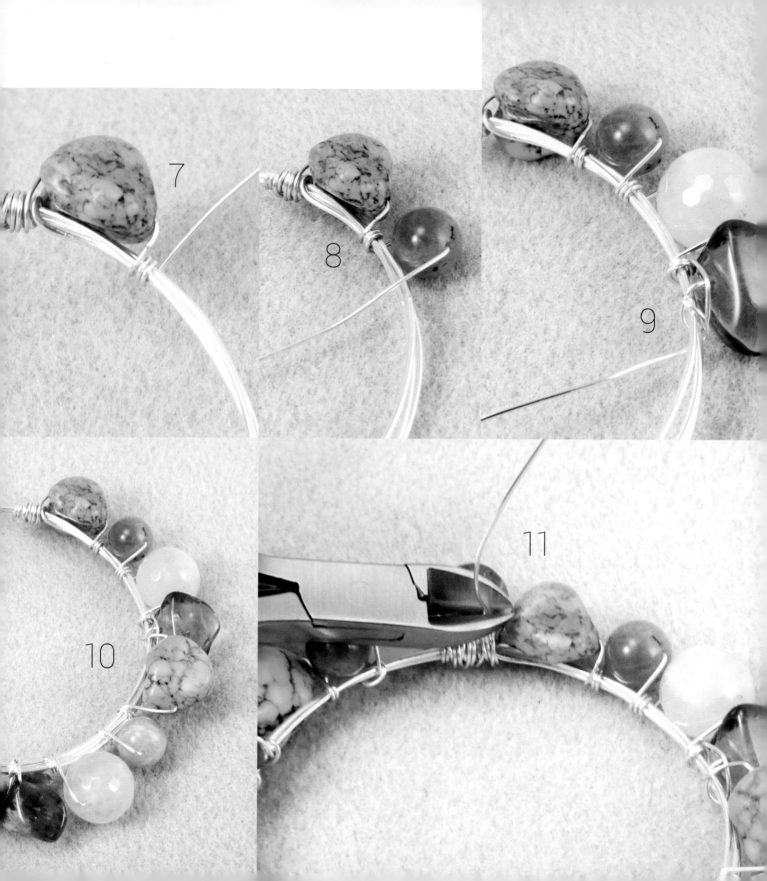

Step 7 While holding the bead firmly in place with one hand, wrap the wire around the bangle base two or three times.

Step 8 Next, thread on your second stone, a round labradorite, and repeat the same process to attach it.

Step 9 Continue around the bangle adding the remaining two stones: a rose quartz and amethyst. As the amethyst nugget is drilled at the bottom of the stone, use the wire to wrap around the stone clockwise once, to secure it in place. The main aim of the wire wrapping is to make a strong and sturdy piece so if it doesn't feel like enough, wrap some more.

Tip *Bangles can take a bashing, so you want to be sure to make this piece nice and strong. Make your wraps tight and if anything is feeling loose, give it an extra wrap for good measure.*

Step 10 Work your way around the bangle adding on the stones one by one.

Step 11 As you approach the end, try to plan it so that you finish at the end of a set of stones; but this will depend on the size of your beads and bangle. Look ahead and plan which stones will go where. You can always add in a bit more wire wrapping if needed. After the final stone, wrap the wire around the base a few extra times and cut with your cutters before squashing the end in.

Tip *Try out different designs with any leftover stones; you don't have to go all the way around the bangle. It works well if you create the round bangle shape, bend a flat section in at one end, and attach a cluster of stones to that bit.*

MOOD BOARD & DESIGN PROCESS

Lace is something that always adds a touch of luxury to
any item, and lace and gold seem particularly luxurious
so I wanted to pair the two in a statement piece. The
small gold beads came to mind when I thought of vintage
dresses with seed pearls worked into embroidered or lace
fabric, encapsulating the luxury in *Downton Abbey* or *The
Great Gatsby*. But lace also has its cheeky side—think frilly
tennis knickers—and that gave me the idea of using lace
from underwear on a cuff.

LUXURY LACE

Easy-to-make, funky lace bracelet

Transform a simple cuff base and a piece of pretty lace into a luxurious, designer-looking piece. Once you have mastered the basics of this simple project, you can adapt the design to really make it your own.

- Medium/large size paintbrush
- Small brush for gluing
- Scissors
- Ruler
- Chain-nose pliers
- Round-nose pliers
- Side cutters

MATERIALS
- Gold acrylic paint
- Brass cuff base
- Sheet of white lace (or can be taken from the back of some new white lacy knickers, the larger the size the better)
- White (PVA) glue
- Thin purple suede, enough to cover cuff
- US 26 guage (SWG 27, 0.4mm) gold-plated wire
- Approx. 60 gold 6mm beads

Step 1 Apply a few layers of the gold acrylic paint to the brass cuff. Make sure you leave the piece to dry after each layer and apply three to four coats of paint to give a nice, solid gold color.

Step 2 Cut out a rectangular sheet of lace that is roughly twice the width and length of the cuff to give you plenty of room to work with.

Step 3 Cover the outside of the cuff in a layer of white (PVA) glue and place the lace on top, making sure you check you are happy with the design of the piece of lace that will cover the front of the bracelet.

Step 4 Curve the lace around so that the cuff's outside edge is covered. Use a paintbrush to dab glue to the outside of the lace and cuff for additional sticking and to make the fabric slightly waterproof. Remember this glue dries clear so you won't see it once it is dry.

Step 5 Cut off any large excess bits of lace and tuck the end in over one side, as shown in the image. Make sure you put a layer of glue on the inside of the cuff before gently folding over the lace with your fingers guiding it into place.

Step 6 Repeat this process on the other side of the piece, cutting down the lace if needed. You want a relatively straight line, but the inside will be covered with suede later so don't worry about getting it perfect.

Step 7 To fold the ends in, apply the glue first to both sides (the lace and the cuff), then fold the lace twice, around the curve in the corner; it's a bit like wrapping a present. If necessary, push the ends down tightly with your fingers and be generous with the glue to get it to stick.

Tip *Check the lace you are using— some lace is very thick, so the gold won't show through very well, and some has lots of gaps so will work better. Some laces are highly patterned with flowers etcetera and others more basic or geometric. Select the style and color you prefer to get the desired effect.*

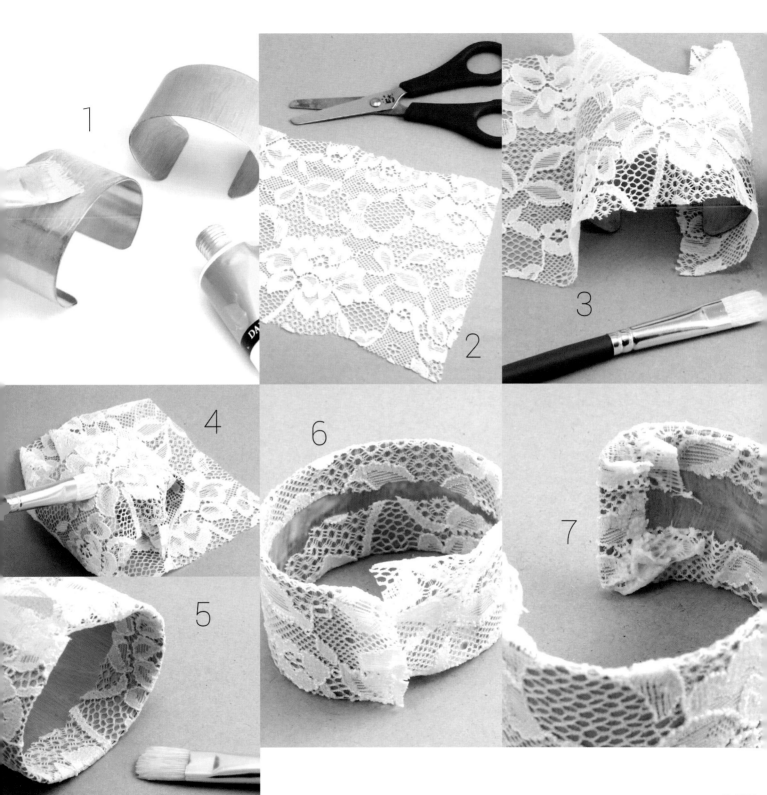

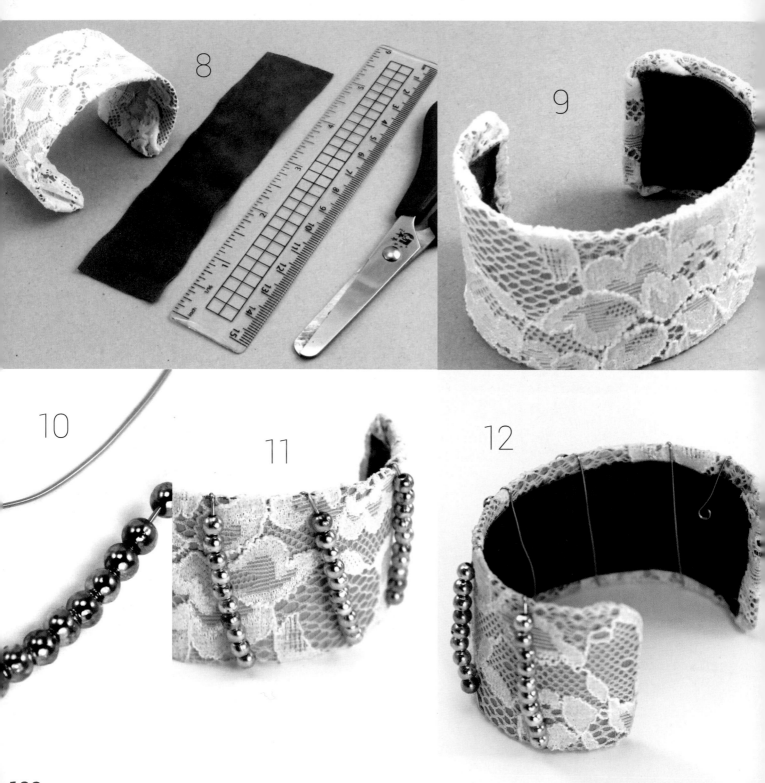

Step 8 Measure out two lengths of purple suede long enough to cover the inside of the cuff.

Step 9 Apply a layer of glue to the underside of one piece of suede and gently place it into position, securing it down on the inside of the cuff. You may need to trim down the ends if it is too long so make any necessary adjustments then leave for all the glue to set.

Step 10 Cut 27³⁄₈in (700mm) of 0.4mm wire and make a loop at one end using the round-nose pliers (see page 26 for detailed instructions). Thread 10 beads on to the wire. Bend the end of the wire with the loop over the top edge of the cuff about ³⁄₈in (10mm) from the end of the cuff and press down with the chain-nosed pliers to secure.

Step 11 Slide the beads along the wire so they sit along the outside of the cuff and wrap the wire round the back of the cuff. Use chain-nosed pliers to press the wire round the edges of the cuff. Add another 10 beads and wrap the cuff again. Continue to wrap and place the beads until there are six lines of beads on the outside.

Step 12 Trim the wire leaving ¾–1¼in (18–28mm) and make a loop on the end. Fold the wire to the back of the cuff and flatten with your pliers. Glue the second piece of suede over the wire to secure it and make the cuff more comfortable

Tip *White (PVA) glue sets clear so there's no need to worry about the white color of it affecting the design. Apply plenty of glue to make sure the piece sticks and to make your cuff more durable.*

MOOD BOARD & DESIGN PROCESS

The starting point for this piece was the theme of Aladdin's cave. Movies can be great sources of inspiration for new collections. I began by looking at golden lamps, rugs, and shoes from this theme and then added in the turquoise and teal-colored fabrics and stones.

From there I looked at a common make-up palette using this color combination before stumbling across this stunning golden flower pendant using turquoise and teal stones.

From the mood board I set about creating my piece and added in golden swirls taken from the look of the engravings and patterns on the lamp to finish.

ALADDIN'S TREASURE

Luxurious jade and golden treasure-trove bracelet

Sometimes you just want color, beads, and a big over-the-top piece that will really make an outfit. This is just the bracelet, inspired by thoughts of all the treasures that make up Aladdin's cave. With a rich mix of teal, golds, and oranges, this design is sure to catch a few eyes. Follow the steps to build up the layers and make a finished piece ready to impress.

· Round-nose pliers
· Chain-nose pliers
· Flat-nose pliers
· Side cutters

MATERIALS
· Packet of gold-plated
jumprings, 5mm
· Packet of gold-plated
jumprings, 8mm
· Thick curb chain, unsoldered
18 x 12mm link size
· Large gold-plated bolt ring or
lobster clasp, ½in (12mm)
· Packet of gold-plated headpins
· 24in (609mm) length of US gauge
20 (SWG 21, 0.8mm) gold-plated wire
· Packet of small gold-plated
round beads, 2mm
· 6 x faceted iridescent teal oval
crystals, 12mm
· 17 x faceted iridescent gold oval
crystals, 12mm
· 34 x faceted rondelle beads in teal
and aqua (17 of each color), 10 x 8mm
· 24 x faceted iridescent small
aqua beads, 3mm
· 24 x faceted light green small
rondel beads, 4mm
· 12 x faceted amber rondelle
beads, 10 x 8mm

Step 1 Close four of the 8mm jumprings using both your chain-nose and flat-nose pliers and thread them on to one of the 8mm open jumprings.

Step 2 Close that jumpring and you should have a basic five-ringed shape. (See page 37 for detailed instructions on closing jumprings.)

Step 3 Close another two 8mm jumprings and thread them on to a 8mm open jumpring.

Step 4 Thread the open 8mm jumpring through two of the original closed 8mm jumprings from step 1 and close it to make an eight-ringed shape. This is a very basic chain mail technique used to make a long thin chain with jumprings.

Step 5 Carry on in this manner, adding two closed 8mm jumprings through a third open 8mm jumpring (as in step 4) each time until you have a full-length of chain that nearly fits around your wrist, leaving a bit of room for a clasp.

Step 6 Take a length of curb chain and use your pliers to open a link where you want to detach the chain. The length of this chain should be slightly more than the chain mail piece you have just made.

Step 7 Using additional 8mm jumprings, attach the chain mail to the thick curb chain at either end.

Step 8 Create a second, identical length of chain mail and attach it to the large link curb chain on the opposite side. This three-chained mix gives a wide base for you to add many beads to.

9

10

11

12

13

14

Step 9 Attach three 8mm jumprings in a row on one end of the chain.

Step 10 Next, use a 5mm jumpring to attach the clasp at the other end. It is advisable to use a bolt ring or lobster clasp for a bracelet this heavy.

Step 11 Now it's time to start attaching beads. Thread a small gold bead followed by a large oval iridescent teal bead onto a headpin.

Step 12 Snip the wire with your side cutters a little above the bead.

Step 13 Make a loop with your round-nose pliers to hold the bead in place (for this technique, see page 38).

Step 14 Repeat this process with all of your beads, putting a small gold bead on first each time.

Tip *Throw caution to the wind and try attaching a random scatter of beads all over the three chains. This can give a surprisingly pretty effect. However, if you are making your work to sell it may be best to stick to a structure so you can recreate it for multiple orders.*

Tip *Ensure all loops you make and all jumprings you close are 100 percent shut so that no beads can escape at any stage.*

Step 15 Attach an oval teal bead to the first link on the curb chain next to the clasp. Attach the bead using a 5mm gold-plated jumpring, opening it, threading it through the loop in the bead and through the chain, then closing it with the chain-nose and flat-nose pliers.

Step 16 Add a teal bead to every second link of chain, making six beads in total.

Step 17 Add five of the large oval gold beads in between the teal ones.

Step 18 You can now add the faceted teal and aqua rondelles. Put one of each on every link in the chain. Place them on opposite sites of the chain link and rotate them along the chain.

Step 19 Now add beads to the outside chain mail sections. Alternate between the large gold and teal rondelle beads with some smaller 3mm aqua beads dotted in the gaps.

Step 20 Repeat this on the other side of the chain mail and you should start to see the bracelet getting bulkier.

15

16

17

18

19

20

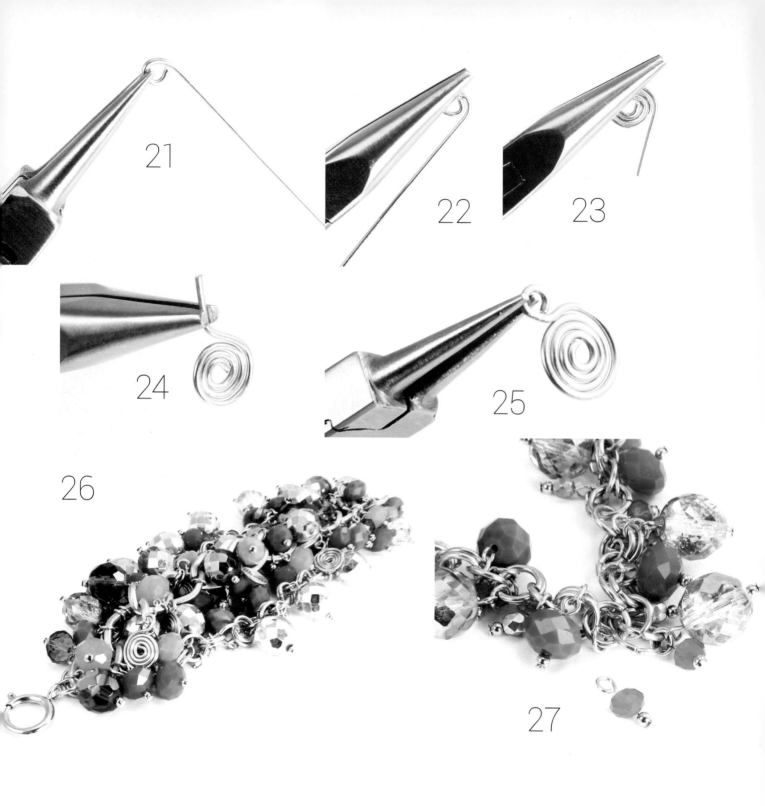

21

22

23

24

25

26

27

Step 21 The next stage is to make a set of swirls to add some wire to the piece. Take a 2in (50mm) length of 20-gauge wire and create a loop at one end.

Step 22 Hold the loop in a pair of chain-nose pliers so that the end of the loop sits at the base of where the pliers grasp the wire. Then gently curve the wire around, using the loop as a guide to build an extra layer of wire on top. After you have completed a quarter circle, move the pliers slightly to catch up with the wire and push round again.

Step 23 Keep moving the pliers round the wire and moving the wire around itself to create the swirl until you have approx. $5/8$in (15mm) of wire remaining.

Step 24 Using your chain-nose pliers, bend the wire so that it is at a right angle to your swirl.

Step 25 Then, using your round-nose pliers, create a loop to the side of the wire. (For detailed instructions on swirl making, see page 42.)

Step 26 Make a total of 12 swirls and add them to your bracelet using a 5mm jumpring, placing one on each of the curb chain links. Also at this stage, add the amber rondelle beads, one to every link on the curb chain.

Step 27 Add the last remaining 4mm light green beads to the two outside chains to finish.

Tip *Take it one step at a time and build up the design. When making designs like this, it is all about the layers. Keep adding beads in rows until you are happy with the design and try it on your wrist at each stage to see how it sits. You may prefer to have fewer beads for a subtler piece or even more, if that's possible!*

MOOD BOARD & DESIGN PROCESS

This mood board started off with the theme of friendship bracelets—a jewelry tradition that has been celebrated for many years. It reminded me of being a child, making them with threads and colorful cords to give to friends for keepsakes. I began by looking at cords and summery, fun color combinations before adding silver charms and other elements, like buttons, to the board. I then got my material box out and started to play around with waxed colored cords and wire before making the bangles. I often find that creating a mood board leads into working with materials and starting to create the piece, which is a great way to progress through your designs.

FRIENDS FOREVER

Trio of colorful charm bangles

Wire is a hugely versatile material and perfect for creating charms. After constructing a solid bangle base covered in colorful cord, you will adorn your piece with jumprings, buttons, feathers, and charms for a fresh summertime look.

TOOLS

- Round-nose pliers
- Chain-nose pliers
- Flat-nose pliers
- Side cutters
- Bead mat (optional)
- Mug, cup, or glass for shaping wire around

MATERIALS

- 39in (1m) silver-plated wire, US gauge 16 (SWG 18, 1.25mm)
- Masking tape
- 78in (2m) per bangle thick-waxed cord in lilac, orange, and pink, ⅛in (2mm) thickness
- White (PVA) glue
- 6 x faceted matte white round beads, 6mm
- 6 x silver-plated headpins
- 6 x small silver-plated jumprings, 6mm
- 45 x large silver-plated jumprings, 10mm
- 1 x silver-plated foldover looped crimp
- Selection of bow, heart, and infinity wire charms (see page 45) plus buttons or beads, and white feather, for decoration

Step 1 Take a length of 16-gauge wire and wrap it around a cup a few times to give it a curved shape. Then put the wire over your wrist and adjust it with your hands to get the desired size of bangle.

Step 2 Apply a piece of masking tape where the wires cross and snip down the wire ends so that there is only a small amount sticking out each end of the masking tape.

Step 3 Make a loop in one end of the wire using the round-nose pliers.

Step 4 Open the loop and tuck it under the wire before closing it shut with your chain-nose pliers. Squeeze down on them to make sure it is a tight fit.

Step 5 Remove the masking tape and repeat this process, making another loop and attaching it to the wire a little way along from the first loop.

Step 6 This completes the wire base for your bangle. For a stacked set, make three of these all the same size.

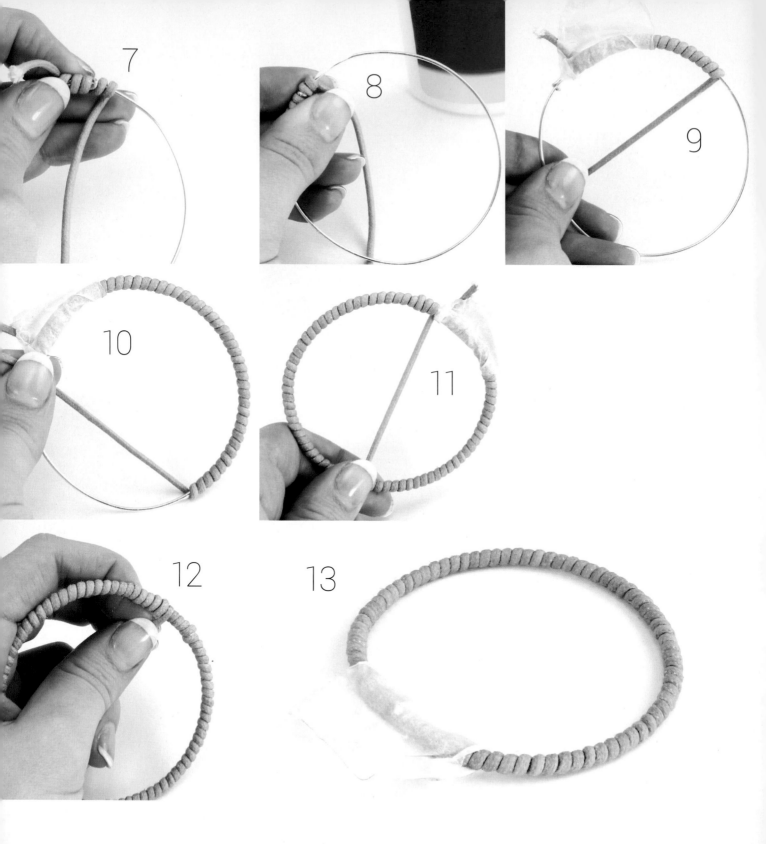

Step 7 Now take a long length of approximately 40–75in (1–2m) of the lilac waxed cord and wrap it around the wire loops a few times either side, holding it in place as you go, leaving a short tail at the beginning.

Step 8 Apply a line of glue to the wire ahead and wrap the cord around the wire tightly and neatly.

Step 9 Once you have done a few wraps, take a piece of masking tape and use it to secure the section that you haven't glued yet.

Step 10 Work your way around the bangle adding in an inch or so of glue to the wire, then making a few wraps, and repeating that process as you work round. Be sure to keep the wire taut and hold it tight with your fingers so that it can't unravel.

Step 11 Glue and wrap your piece all the way to the end. Hold the cord in place and snip it down. Use plenty of glue underneath to stick it in place.

Step 12 Remove the masking tape and go back to glue and wrap the starting section with the end you started with, pulling the cord tightly and wrapping all the way up to meet the other end of the cord in order to cover all the wire.

Step 13 Apply a little extra glue to this joining area and snip the end off the cord so that the two sides meet. This can get a bit messy; try to keep it as neat as possible but remember you will also be covering it with jumprings and charms. Once the glue has been generously applied, put a piece of masking tape over the joining area and allow the glue to set for a few hours.

Tip *It's easy to say, but you want to try and use just enough glue for the cord to be firmly secured to the wire but not so much that it goes everywhere. If in doubt try a practice piece first.*

Step 14 When dry, remove the masking tape and attach a white bead to either side of the messy joining area, allowing 1¹/₄in (31mm) between each bead. To do this, put the white bead on a headpin, cut down, and make a loop at the end using round-nose pliers. Using a 6mm jumpring, thread the looped bead on and close the jumpring around the bracelet. The jumpring is tight and should hold the bead in place. If it doesn't, slightly cut down the jumpring with your cutters and close it until it holds in place on the bangle.

Step 15 Next add 15 x 10mm jumprings to the space in between the white beads. I have made my own jumprings (see page 37 for instructions on how to do this).

Step 16 Attach a white feather to the middle jumpring using a cord end (for instructions on attaching feathers, see steps 1 and 2 on page 66).

Step 17 Finally, add your bow wire charm and a small lilac button with a jumpring attached. Repeat the same process to make the matching two bangles, adding their own wire charms, beads, buttons, feathers, and any other decorative elements you like.

Tip *Play around with the designs– like all the projects in this book, it's most exciting when you can give the pieces your own flavor. Experiment with different charm shapes, buttons, feathers, or other bits and pieces to give your piece a unique design.*

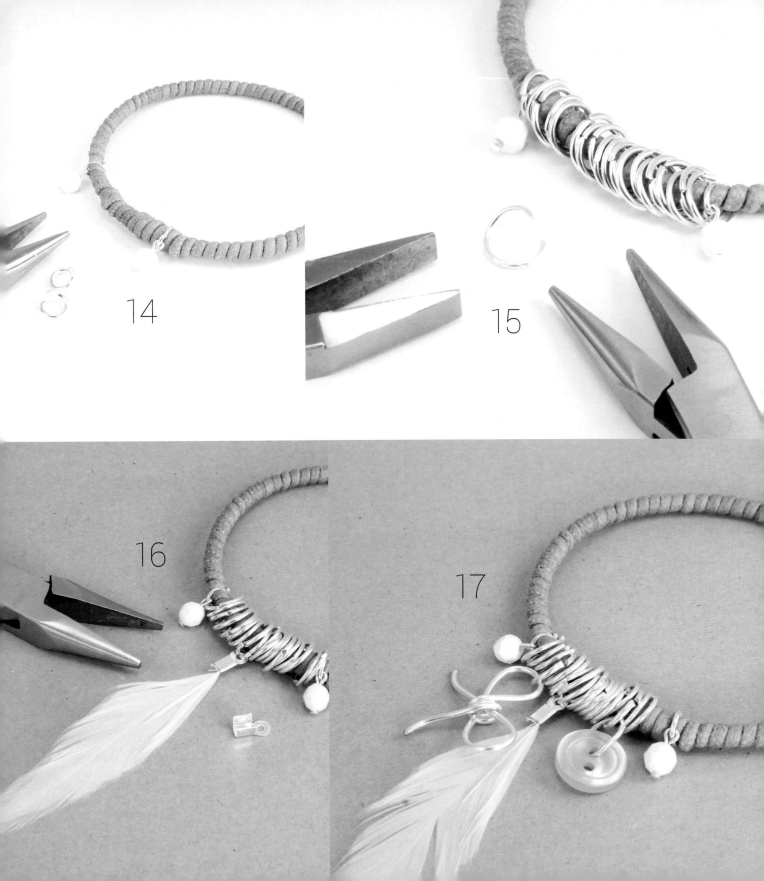

14

15

16

17

Blinging
RINGS

MOOD BOARD & DESIGN PROCESS

When designing this piece I started with the rocks.
I looked at different types of rough, chunky crystals
and rocks, and considered ways I could include them
in a ring that would make a statement but still be
comfortable enough to wear. I then began to look
at gold rocks and clear crystals, and thought of using
metallic paint to create a contrast in my piece. I finished
off the mood board by looking at how these colors have
been used in fashion and nature, before getting to work
creating the wire structure of the ring.

DESTINY

Chunky stone ring wrapped in wire

Get the Midas touch with this wire-based ring that combines a rough quartz stone with a coat of metallic paint. After creating a basic wire base, you will learn to attach the quartz rock bead securely to make a ring that would work well as a statement party piece or to glam up a simple daytime look.

TOOLS

• Paintbrush
• Wooden mandrel (or other object such as a glue stick, for shaping wire)
• Chain-nose pliers
• Side cutters

MATERIALS

• White quartz rock bead
• Gold metallic acrylic paint (and mix of silver and copper paints for additional rings)
• Approx. 52in (132cm) gold-plated wire, US 22 gauge (SWG 22, 0.6mm)

Step 1 Take your chosen bead, lay it on a piece of paper, and paint half of it with the gold paint. Try to paint a straight line to be in keeping with the geometric look. Leave the paint to dry and, if needed, apply a few coats.

Step 2 Take approximately 12in (305mm) of wire and wrap it around the wooden mandrel four or five times. Wrap it at the point on the mandrel that is a little bigger (about two sizes, mark the mandrel first if this helps) than your ring size.

Step 3 Once you have wrapped the wire, take it off the mandrel. Hold it in place with one hand and use the other hand to wrap one end of the wire around the bundle. Wrap three or four times to group the wires together. Try to make your wraps as close to each other and neat as possible.

Step 4 Repeat this wrapping process on the other side of your ring (approximately a third of the way round), again wrapping a few times to make the ring base tight and secure.

Step 5 Cut off both ends with the side cutters and tuck in any sharp edges using chain-nose pliers. You now have a basic wire ring, which should be a size or two bigger than you want the final ring to be.

Step 6 Now take a 40in (1m) length of the wire and attach it to your ring by wrapping it around one of the wraps you have already done. Wrap it four to five times to secure it in place and cut off the short end. Squash in any remaining sharp ends. You should now have a ring base with a long wire attached to it.

Tip *The hardest thing about this ring is getting it to fit. The size will get smaller as you go along wrapping wire around the edges, so make it at least one whole size too big to start with. If it doesn't fit first time you can always remake it, or use for another finger.*

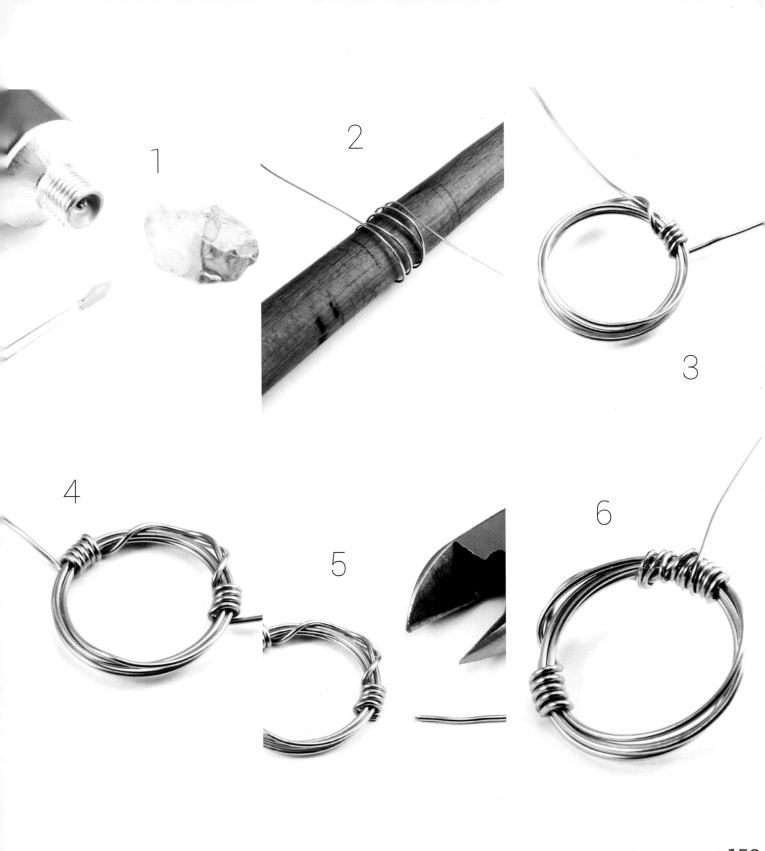

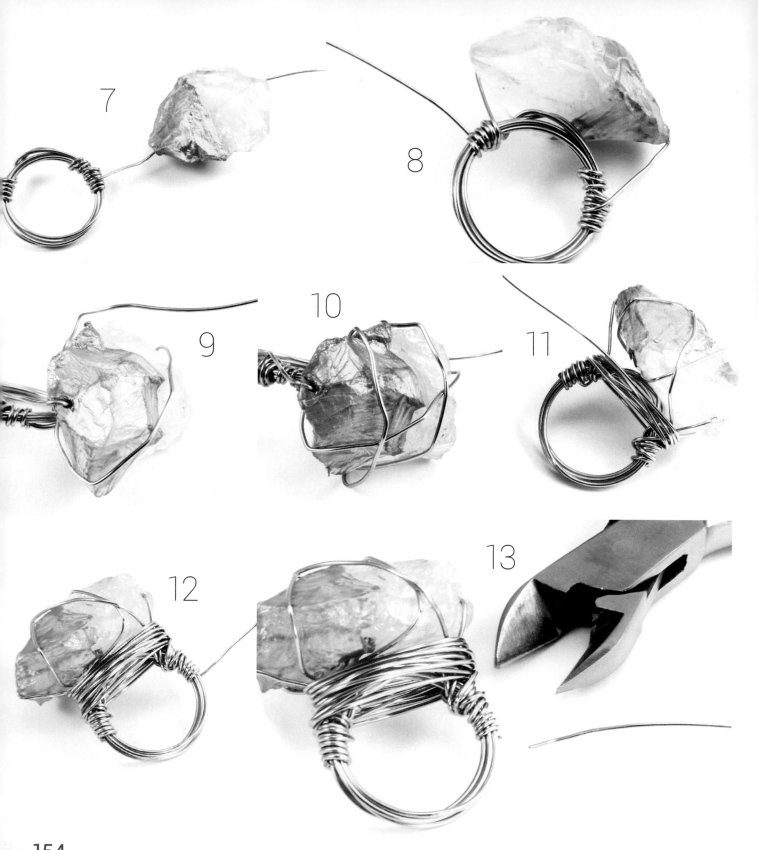

Step 7 Thread your half-painted quartz bead onto the wire, leaving a gap of approximately ⅝in (15mm) between the bead and the ring base.

Step 8 Bend the wire around so that the bead sits at the front of the ring, centered between the two original wraps on the ring base. Adjust the bead as much as needed at this stage to get it in a good position, then wrap the end of the wire around the other side of the ring a few times

Step 9 Wrap the same piece of wire diagonally around the front of the bead and then back up through the other side, making sure not to let the wire go inside the ring base at any stage because this is where your finger will be.

Step 10 Wrap the wire around the bead a few more times until you are happy with the design.

Step 11 Next, wrap the wire clockwise around the back of the bead a few times to fill any gaps (try on the ring to make sure it still fits).

Step 12 When you come to the end of the wire, take it over to the opposite side of the ring from where you started wrapping and make a few finals wraps around the ring base to secure everything in place.

Step 13 Cut off the end and squash the sharp edge in to finish.

T|p *Use silver and copper paints with silver, copper or gold wires to make a set of metallic chunky rings. You could even have one for each finger!*

MOOD BOARD & DESIGN PROCESS

Candy as a starting point for jewelry? Why not? Maybe I was just hungry today but I wanted to make some fun rings starting with candy as my theme. Sometimes we get too serious about our designs and just need to play.

I began by looking at the traditional candy jewelry bracelets and thought about making a ring version using similar-style beads. I then used the mood board to think of color combinations and added in the use of charms before getting to work making my first piece.

CANDY

Colorful, stretchy charm rings

Take inspiration from the candy store and whip up a batch of charm rings using a stack of colorful beads, a few silver charms, and a little elastic. The perfect pieces for making and selling your jewelry or giving to friends, these easy rings cost almost nothing and are easy to make.

MATERIALS
• Stretchy nylon cord,
$1/32$in (1mm) thick
• Silver plated jumprings,
$1/4$in (6mm)
• Selection of silver-plated charms,
approx. $5/8$in (15mm) in size
• Small $3/16$in (4mm) stacked pink
beads (also in purple and turquoise for
additional rings) and with a hole
big enough to insert cord

Step 1 Choose the charm you want to sit at the front of your ring, such as this silver-plated heart, and attach it to a small jumpring and close.

Step 2 Thread the jumpring charm on to the middle of a length of stretchy nylon cord of approximately 8in (20cm) to give yourself extra length to work with.

Step 3 Next, thread your beads on to the nylon on one side of the charm. Make sure the beads that you use have a hole in the middle that is large enough to fit over the nylon.

Step 4 Continue adding your beads on the other side of the central charm.

Step 5 When you have threaded on enough beads to go around your finger, pull the two ends of the nylon together and tie four knots in the thread. Make each of the knots progressively tighter, with the first one being quite light and pulling really tightly by the last to make sure it is strong and durable.

Step 6 Cut off any excess nylon and your ring is all ready to wear.

Tip *The great thing about making these rings with stretchy nylon cord is that you don't have to worry about the size being exact as they will stretch to fit any finger.*

1

2

3

4

5

6

MOOD BOARD & DESIGN PROCESS

As you can probably tell by now, I use color as a starting point for a lot of my pieces. Oddly enough the idea for this piece came from eating green and purple grapes, which made me think how striking the two colours can look together and I set about creating a mood board around this. I had some teal green mounted crystals in my bead cupboard, so I thought of adding crystals to the mix, which took the theme down a more glam-rock, statement ring path. The progression of your designs from start to finish can sometimes surprise you; I know I often end up making something very different to what I originally had in mind, but love the end piece just as much.

GLAMOUR

Star-shaped glam-rock ring

Made with vibrant green flat-backed crystals sitting on purple suede and black leather, this Seventies-style ring is a great beginners' project. It would look perfect matched with a pretty single-colored dress—or even better, those tight black leather trousers!

TOOLS

- Cup or thin mug, as template
- Pen or pencil
- Fabric-cutting scissors

MATERIALS

- Black leather
- Thin purple suede
- UHU or other strong fabric glue
- Superglue or a two-part epoxy resin
- 1 x rectangular flat-backed mounted crystal, ¾ x ½in (18 x 12mm)
- 8 x teardrop flat-backed mounted crystals, ⅜in (10mm)
- Silver-plated ring blank

Step 1 Lay out the black leather and draw round the base of a cup or thin mug to create a circle template for the front of your ring.

Step 2 Use sharp fabric scissors to neatly cut out the circle.

Step 3 Repeat this on the piece of thin purple suede.

Step 4 Use a strong glue like UHU to stick the two pieces together. The purple side is going to be the front of your ring and the black leather the back.

Step 5 Take a rectangular flat-backed crystal and glue it in to the center of the purple suede.

Tip *This ring is quite delicate due to it being made with glue and suede. If you find that the ring blank at the back comes off after a few wears, glue a strip of thin black suede vertically over where the ring blank is attached to the back of the piece and leave to set. This will reinforce the join. Bear in mind that this piece is perfect for a few fun nights but it won't last for ever.*

Step 6 Next, gently glue on two of the teardrop-shaped mounted flat-backs, one at the top and one at the bottom of the rectangle, pointing outward.

Step 7 Glue two more teardrops on, placing each at the center of the long sides of the rectangular crystal.

Tip *If the glue is going everywhere, it can help to apply it gradually, using a cocktail stick, which gives you a bit more control.*

Step 8 Add the remaining teadrops to the four gaps in between the four you have already glued in place. Then set aside for a few hours to dry.

Step 9 To finish, use a strong glue such as Superglue to attach a ring blank on the back. Allow 24 hours to set before wearing.

MOOD BOARD & DESIGN PROCESS

Cocktail rings are one of my favorite styles of jewelry so I had lots of fun with this mood board. I began by collecting pictures and cuttings of some lovely rings and noticed a trend for stacking rings on one finger. I thought about whether to create three separate rings with different stones on but decided on making a piece that looked as though it could be three rings but was actually just one, big statement ring. I looked at different color combinations and thought about the kind of ring you might wear out on a glamorous shopping trip or on an adventure around town. Then I got down to making.

ENTWINED

Stunning three-layered cocktail ring

Combine the subtlety of semiprecious rose quartz and labradorite
with the rich tones of amethyst and gold wire wraps to make this classy cocktail ring.
Surprisingly quick to make, using a few fundamental tools and techniques
anyone can make this piece at home.

- Wooden ring mandrel (or glue stick to shape wire around)
- Side cutters
- Round-nose pliers
- Chain-nose pliers

MATERIALS

- 60in (1.5m) Us 20 gauge (SWG 21, 0.8mm) gold-plated wire
- 20mm round, faceted rose quartz bead
- 10mm round labradorite bead
- 18mm oval, faceted amethyst flat bead

Step 1 Cut off a 60in (1.5m) length of 20-gauge wire and thread the rose quartz bead on one end, placing it about 4½in (115mm) along the wire. Put a ring or ring-sizer on the wooden mandrel (or other round object of the right size) and make a small mark where it sits.

Step 2 Place the bead on the mandrel (or similar-shaped object) and wrap the wire in both directions around the mandrel so that you have one piece on top and the other underneath the bead.

Step 3 You now need to make sure the bead and wires are at the part of the ring mandrel that will fit your ring size. So line the bead up with the mark made in step 1. Then bend the wires at right angles so that they face up and down either side of the bead, as shown in the image.

Step 4 Wrap the wires clockwise around the side of the bead on opposite sides until you have covered the gap between the bead and the ring base.

Step 5 Take the ring off the mandrel at this stage and move one of the ends of wire to one side of the ring circle.

Step 6 Make a few wraps here to secure it in place.

Tip *Make sure you use a nice thick wire for this piece as it serves to create the settings around the stones and creates space in between each one to give a stacked ring effect.*

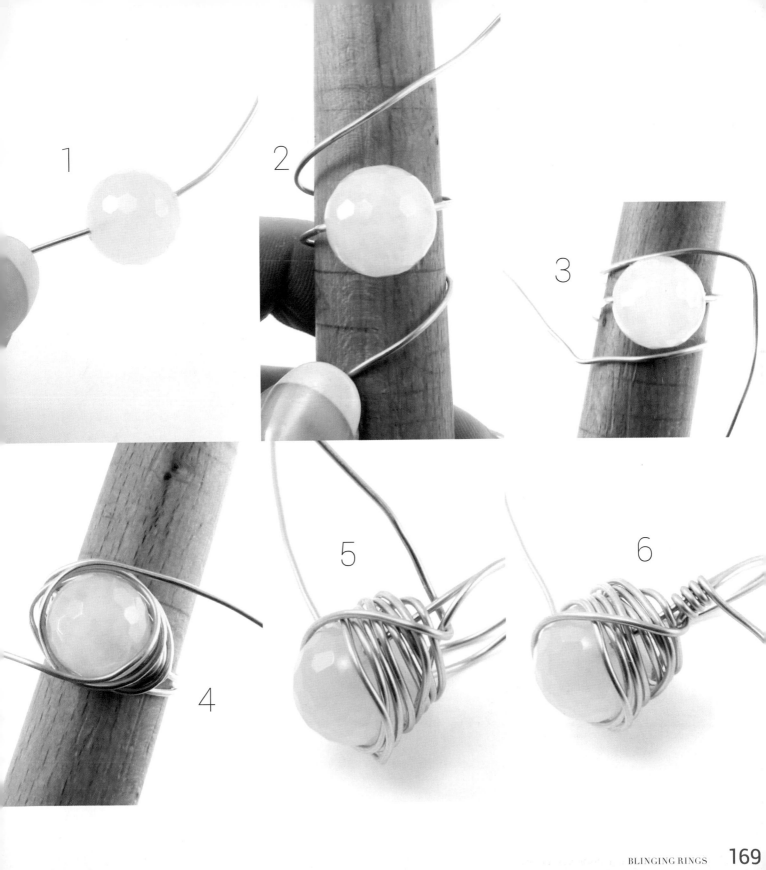

Step 7 Cut off any excess wire on this side, leaving ¾in (19mm) spare at the end.

Step 8 Use the ¾in (19mm) of wire to make a mini swirl to finish this side of the ring (for making swirls, see page 42).

(for making swirls, see page 42)

Step 9 Next, thread your labradorite bead on to the end of the long piece of wire and place it at the top left side of the rose quartz bead.

Tip *When adding the second and third bead, be sure to place them in the correct space so that the overall design is how you want it.*

Step 10 Begin wrapping the wire around the bead counterclockwise.

Step 11 Continue wrapping until you have created a complete wire-wrapped setting for your stone.

Step 12 Thread on the third and final bead, the oval amethyst, and place it to the right of the labradorite bead and above the rose quartz.

Step 13 Wrap the wire around the bead in the same way as above, to create a wire setting for it to sit in.

Step 14 Wrap the wire a few times back around the rose quartz bead and ring circle at the back to make sure it is all firmly held in place.

Step 15 To finish, wrap the end of the wire around the remaining side of the ring, cut off any excess and create a swirl.

Tip *This ring usually comes up a bit bigger than planned, so try using a smaller size position on the mandrel to start with. If in doubt, make a practice ring first. The more you make, the easier they become.*

SUPPLIERS AND RESOURCES

UK

Beads Direct
Unit 10, Duke Street
Loughborough
LE11 1ED
+44 (0) 1509 218028
www.beadsdirect.co.uk

**Beadworks Bead Shop
(Covent Garden)**
21a Tower Street
Covent Garden
London
WC2H 9NS
+44(0) 207 240 0931
www.beadworks.co.uk

The Bead Shop (Manchester)
1st Floor, 52 Church Street
Manchester
M4 1PW
+44 (0) 161 833 9950
www.the-beadshop.co.uk

Bellore/Rashbells
39 Greville Street
London
EC1N 8PJ
+44(0) 207 404 3220
www.bellore.co.uk

Cookson Gold
59–83 Victoria Street
Birmingham
B1 3N
+44 (0) 845 100 1122
www.cooksongold.com

Creative Beadcraft
1 Marshal Street
London
W1F 9BA
+44 (0) 20 7734 1982
www.creativebeadcraft.co.uk

Fred Aldous
37 Lever Street
Manchester
M1 1LW
+44 (0) 161 236 4224
www.fredaldous.co.uk

HS Walsh
44 Hatton Garden
London
EC1N 8ER
+44 (0) 20 7242 3711
www.hswalsh.com

International Craft
Unit 4, The Empire Centre
Imperial Way
Watford
WD24 4YH
+44 (0) 1923 235336
www.internationalcraft.com

Wires.co.uk
Unit 3, Zone A, Chelmsford Road
Industrial Estate
Great Dunmow
CM6 1HD
+44(0) 1371 238013
www.wires.co.uk

USA

Art Beads.com
11901 137th Ave Ct. KPN
Gig Harbor
Washington 98329
1-253-857-3433
www.artbeads.com

Bead Palace Inc.
163 South Madison Ave
Greenwood
Indiana 46142
www.beadpalaceinc.com

Beadaholique
www.beadaholique.com

Fire Mountain Gems
1 Fire Mountain Way
Grants Pass
1-800-355-2137
www.firemountaingems.com

Fusion Beads
3830 Stone Way N
Seattle
WA 98103
1-206-782-4595
www.fusionbeads.com

Happy Mango Beads
PO Box 64
Berthoud
CO 80513
970-532-2546
www.happymangobeads.com

JewelrySupply.com
www.jewelrysupply.com
866-380-746

Para Wire
2-8 Central Ave
East Orange
NJ 07018
973-672-0500
www.parawire.com

Rio Grande
7500 Bluewater Rd
NW Albuquerque
NM 87121
1-800-545-6566
www.riogrande.com

Shipwreck Beads
8560 Commerce Place Dr NE.
Lacey
WA 98516
(800)-950-4232
www.shipwreckbeads.com

ABOUT THE AUTHOR

Jessica Rose is the award-winning founder of **JewelryFromHome.com** and the **London Jewellery School**, one of the world's largest jewelry training centers.

She set up the business aged just 21 in 2009 with only one class a month from a community hall in south London. Now the school is a huge success, having trained over 9,000 students and running hundreds of fun and professional jewelry classes each year.

Jessica fell in love with jewelry making when she took her first class back in 2004. She began teaching in 2008 and hasn't looked back.

She specializes in beaded fashion jewelry and is also passionate about jewelry businesses, having supported many people setting up and running their own home-based jewelry start-ups.

To find out more visit: **www.londonjewelleryschool.co.uk** or **www.jewelryfromhome.com**

PICTURE ACKNOWLEDGMENTS

Images listed below are from iStock/Thinkstock. All other images are by Jessica Rose.

p52: Alexey Khromushin, akit, AnjelaGr, Anmfoto, Audrius Priveda, dinachi, Eduardo Jose Bernardino, Elnur Amikishiyev/Hemera/Thinkstock, largeformat4x5, Lessa Dar, Maria esau, sprokop.

p58: Elnur Amikishiyev, KRproductions, Jasmin Awad, kokoroyuki, Lalouetto, Ruth Black, Tom Gowanlock.

p64: Enskanto, Evgenii Karamyshev/Hemera/Thinkstock, Guzel Karimova, geniebird, Ketian Chen, mjf795, Lalouetto, Oleg Gekman, robbiverte.

p70: Anmfoto, Avrorra, Carla Donofrio/Hemera/Thinkstock, forever63, Kannaa, Lalouetto, leadlciceraro, yigit deniz özdemir.

p78: florin1961, Gromovataya, Ingram Publishing/Thinkstock, Gromovataya, Iuliia Azarova, Nadezda Korobkova, Olga Zaretskaya, Zoonar/N.Okhitin/Zoonar/Thinkstock.

p88: fergregory, forever63, Hemera Technologies/PhotoObjects.net/Thinkstock, kosmos111, Maryia Bahutskaya, Reid Dalland, Silmen, Zoonar/homydesign/Zoonar/Thinkstock.

p94: Antonio Balaguer soler/Hemera/Thinkstock, Evgeniy Glazov/iStock, flytosky11, Jirawat Jerdjamrat, nschatzi, Olga Miltsova/Hemera/Thinkstock, sundrawalex/iStock.

p98: DelafrayeNicolas, ITkach, Jack Hollingsworth/Photodisc/Thinkstock, Lalouetto, Joanna-Palys, littleevilyorky, ratmaner, Reimphoto, Ron Chapple Stock/Ron Chapple Studios/Thinkstock.

p104: alblec, Avrorra, Brian McEntire, Colin Walton/Thinkstock, heckmannoleg, Hemera Technologies/PhotoObjects.net/Getty Images/Thinkstock, markrhiggins, poplasen, Tajarja.

p114: adam mangold, ariwasabi, Medioimages/Photodisc/Thinkstock, mika makkonen, moodboard/Thinkstock, Photos.com/©Getty Images/Thinkstock, planinasum,Tracy Hebden, XiXinXing.

p118: Alesikka, EmilyPackard, Joanna-Palys, La Corivo, Mallivan, Rasulovs, ShaunWilkinson, VvoeVale, Wavebreakmedia Ltd/Wavebreak Media/Thinkstock, Yarygin.

p124: Chelnok, IuriiSokolov, Fekete Zoltßn/Hemera/Thinkstock, longtaildog, MagMos, MagMos/iStock/Thinkstock, Momo64, Ruslan Bosikov/Hemera/Thinkstock, Viktoriia Kulish/Hemera/Thinkstock, Zametalov.

p130: Chimpinski, David MacLurg, fergregory, Joanna-Palys, Iurii Osadchyi, neurodominator, Philip Lange, Simone Andress, Voyagerix, VvoeVale;

p140: Geo-grafika, hawk111, Jupiterimages/Photos.com/Getty Images/Thinkstock, KayTaenzer, mamadela, oksix, Rinky Dink Images/Eyecandy Images/Thinkstock, vesmil.

p150: bigjohn36, Fruit Cocktail, gebai, Igor Boldyrev, Jupiterimages/Goodshoot/Getty Images/Thinkstock, olgakr, TonyLomas, ValuaVitaly, VvoeVale, wertorer.

p156: alisbalb, belchonock, Creatas Images (Creatas/Thinkstock), Fuse/Thinkstock, Jupiterimages/Creatas/Getty Images/Thinkstock, Jupiterimages/Pixland/Thinkstock, Jupiterimages/Polka Dot/Thinkstock, Nikhil Gangavane/Hemera/Thinkstock, MilaSemenova, Serezniy.

p160: Aeya, boggy22, Design Pics/Tomas del Amo, florin1961, janniwet, MonicaSantosHerberg, Purestock, sommaiphoto.

p166: 97, Aeya, Eugene Bochkarev, Judson Abts, MalyDesigner, manyakotic, TPopova, Vladimir Nikulin, Zeynep Özyürek.

INDEX

A

adhesives — 22
Aladdin's treasure — 131–9

B

Beach babe — 119–23
bead mat — 14
beads — 17
bicones — 17
bow charm — 46
bracelets
    Aladdin's treasure — 131–9
    Beach babe — 119–23
    Friends forever — 141–7
    Love hurts — 115–17
    Luxury lace — 125–9
briolettes — 17, 41
buttons — 22

C

cabochons — 22
Candy — 157–9
chain — 22
Chain attraction — 71–7
chain-nose pliers — 14
Chanel, Coco — 8
charms — 18
clasps — 18, 33
coils, making — 34
Coral glow — 53–7

cord ends — 18
crimps — 18, 49
crystals, flat-backed — 22

D

Destiny — 151–5

E

earrings
    Fiesta — 89–93
    Pearl luster — 95–7
    Purple haze — 105–11
    Spring burst — 99–103
earwires — 18, 30
elements — 18
Entwined — 167–71

F

fabric — 22
feathers — 22
Fiesta — 89–93
findings — 18
    metal types — 21
flat-backed mounted gems — 22
flat-nose pliers — 14
Forbidden glamour — 79–85
Friends forever — 141–7

G

Glamour — 161–5
glues — 22

H

headpins — 18, 38
heart charm — 45

I

infinity charm — 46

J

jumprings — 18, 37

L

loops, making — 26
    headpins — 38
Love hurts — 115–17
Luxury lace — 125–9

M

masking tape — 22
metal types — 21
mood boards — 10
mugs — 14

N

necklaces
    Chain attraction — 71–7
    Coral glow — 53–7

Forbidden glamour 79–85
Paradise 65–9
Sea breeze 59–63
needle files 14
nylon cord 21

P

paintbrushes 14
paints 22
Paradise 65–9
Pearl luster 95–7
pliers 14
Purple haze 105–11
PVA glue 22

R

rings
Candy 157–9
Destiny 151–5
Entwined 167–71
Glamour 161–5
rondelle beads 17
round-nose pliers 14

S

scissors 14
Sea breeze 59–63
seed beads 17

selling jewelry 11
side cutters 14
Spring burst 99–103
steel block and hammer 14
stretchy nylon/elastic 21
stringing materials 21
superglue 22
swirls, making 42

T

threading beads with wire 29
tools 14
trend spotting 9

U

UHU 22

W

waxed cord 21
white (PVA) glue 22
wire 18
    metal types 21
wire charms 45–6
wire wrapping
    briolettes 41
    headpins 38
wooden mandrel 14

To place an order, or to request a catalogue, contact:
GMC Publications, Castle Place, 166 High Street, Lewes, East Sussex, BN7 1XU United Kingdom
Tel: +44 (0)1273 488005
www.gmcbooks.com